10329

D0896443

PHOENIX FIRST ASSEMBLY
13613 N. Cave Creek Rd.
Phoenix, AZ 85022

Library
Oakland S.U.M.

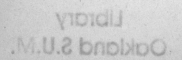
Library
Oakland S.U.M.

BIOG
LUN

8/6/85

Lowell

Compiled by
Ken Scrivner

PHOENIX FIRST ASSEMBLY
13613 N. Cave Creek Rd.
Phoenix, AZ 85022

Lowell Lundstrom Ministries, Inc.
Sisseton, South Dakota 57262

Copyright © 1979 by Lowell Lundstrom Ministries, Inc.
Sisseton, South Dakota 57262

First Printing November 1979
Second Printing February 1981

ISBN O-938220-15-2

Library of Congress Catalog Card Number
77-075458

ALL RIGHTS RESERVED

PRINTED IN THE UNITED STATES OF AMERICA

CONTENTS

PREFACE

A reward should be given to my team members for their years of sacrificial labor.

1st to my gentle and loving wife, Connie, who has been by my side in the ministry, sacrificing 22 years to live on the highway even while rearing a family.

2nd to my children, Londa, Lisa, Lowell Jr. and Lance, who have been so helpful in God's work and patient to share the heavy responsibilities of the ministry.

3rd to my brother, Larry, and his wife, Gloria, and their children, LaShawn, LaDawn and Lee Donavan, who have been faithful partners with us in God's work. Connie and I will never forget the effort Larry and Gloria have made.

4th to Leon and Ronda and little Larissa, who are some of the most hard-working troopers to work in evangelism.

5th to Mom and Dad Lundstrom for their years of help and encouragement. For nearly twenty years Mom has carried the load of our office while Dad has been willing to run the farm while she was at work and his sons were on the road.

6th to Bud and Alice Brown. Mom Brown has been one of the most faithful workers any leader could ever have and the best mother-in-law in the world.

7th to people like Jack Trosen, Bruce Schoeman, Carl Malz, Chet and Carol Priewe, Mark Anderson, Ed and Fern Arness, Max Albert, Don Kooy, Larry Strom, Eldon Babcock, Steve Eskelson, Joe Gruber, Al Frisinger, Irv Slaamot, John Poore, Dave Drach, Kevin Hudson, Dave Koechel, John Peterson, Don Thompson, Willard Mason, Jim

Kerby, Ken Scrivner, Nancy Fall, Jerry McClure, Christopher Watson, Jane Reyhons, Reuben Njaa, Chris Ward, Steve Booher, Paul Secord, Everett Hind, Carl Johnson, Gladwin Kjosa, Robert Hanson, Olaf ("Dad") Hanson, Glen Brooks, Walter Bennett, Ted Dienert, Jesse Peterson, Bob Daney, Lyle and Hilda Thorpe, Steve Vaudrey, Marsha Bumpous, Bette Dalberg, Elaine German, Deloria Reyelts, Helen Ready, Ardella Kelly, Lavonne Mattson, Marlene Worthly, Karen Eytzen, Evelyn Benson, Julia Hills, Marilyn Backman, Carol Fitz, Marsha Lynch, Gail Pearson, Rob Mumm, Elaine Herniman and a host of others.

8th, and especially, our partners and friends, who have prayed and given to this work of God, who have been the body, arms, legs and fingers of this ministry.

Although attention may be given to me, as a person's head is featured in a photograph, the head knows that without the body and its willingness the head would never make it. May God bless these people (and please forgive me if I have missed any) who have enabled me in my weakness to be a blessing.

Sincerely in Christ,

Lowell

Lowell Lundstrom
Sisseton, South Dakota

Lowell

1.

God, I Wish I Could Know You

My roots go deep into the South Dakota sod. My grandmother, Christine Matson, was reared in a log cabin in Minnesota. My grandfather, Adolf Lundstrom, came to Minnesota from Sweden and married Christine. They chose the prairies of South Dakota as their new home.

The farm they bought had been in Indian territory. They built a little house and braved the icy winds that blew out of the northern plains. They had seven children. My father was the youngest.

As a small boy, he remembered the two-by-two missionaries who would come to share the Gospel. They were so named because they went out in pairs, lived an austere life and never married. My grandmother became a godly woman. While her doctrine was a little legalistic, it was nevertheless quite fundamental. She was a real saint.

From the earliest moment of my life I remember God speaking to me. I know it was because of my grandmother's continual prayers. I remember God speaking to me when I was about 7. My grandmother had given me a book containing the birth, death and life of Jesus Christ. When I read about Jesus dying in my place it gripped me so that I began to cry. My folks heard my sobbing and asked what was wrong. I couldn't explain it. I said, "Nothing is wrong." So I just held a pillow over my head and cried myself to sleep. I loved Jesus from the very first moment.

Lowell Lundstrom

WHEN Lowell was a tiny thing, he showed signs of being a strong-willed individual. I remember having to discipline him, and instead of spanking him I'd hold him on my lap for a long time. I'd hold him and rock him sometimes for an hour at a time. He was never disobedient except when he was self-willed. Generally he was quite obedient and wasn't one to get into mischief much.

As a small child he seemed to play with children older than himself, and one day he got into some trouble with some of the boys. Of course he came home with his problem, and we sent him right out there again to take care of his own battles. Right from the beginning we encouraged him. He was pretty self-confident, and we did what we could to encourage that trait.

Lawrence Lundstrom
Lowell's father

Even though my parents weren't active Christians, I've always been thankful for their good, solid moral training. Mom was reared Catholic, and she had a tremendous fear of God. My dad was a Protestant, but he wasn't protesting against anything. The only time I remember hearing prayer in our home was when there was an electrical storm. Nobody ever prayed before our meals; but let me tell you, when those tremendous electrical storms would come and lightning would crash all around the house, my mom would say, "God help us, God help us," and run for the cellar. But they taught my brothers and me how to work hard, and they taught us honesty, and I will forever be indebted to them for that.

Lowell

LOWELL was quite interested in sports as a small child. We lived in Minneapolis next to a park which had some hills. I got him a pair of skis, and there was a doctor who took an interest in teaching 5-year-old Lowell how to ski. In short order Lowell was skiing quite well for his age.

He wasn't so fortunate at steering his wagon. He was at the park coasting down the hill, and he fell off the wagon and broke out all four of his front teeth.

Another time he was coasting down a hill, and I was watching him from the window. I thought, "Boy, that is a long hill," and I saw there was one lone tree in front of Lowell. I thought, "Surely he won't hit that tree," but sure enough, he hit it square and broke his collarbone.

Lawrence Lundstrom

Dad was a machinist during World War II, and we lived in Minneapolis. When his health began to fail we decided it would be best to move back to where he grew up as a boy, my grandparents' home near Peever, South Dakota. We began to farm the land.

Lowell

I had Lowell and Larry working on the farm at an early age. Lowell was sort of the manager, and he was quite ambitious. Larry didn't care if he finished his work or not, so Lowell sort of served as the ramrod. I loved to hunt, and so when Lowell and Larry would finish their chores we'd go hunting for those big Canadian ducks and geese. By the time they were 7 or 8, they'd be helping me rake hay and drive the tractor in the fields.

Lawrence Lundstrom

I remember other times when I felt the Spirit of God. I used to watch people going to church on a Sunday morning. We'd be out hunting or working on the farm, and I would say to myself, "I wish our family would serve the Lord." I remember going through the fields and looking up at the clouds and the beauty of the sky, and I remember praying, "God, I wish I could know you."

I remember God speaking to me another time as a student in a small one-room schoolhouse. The Gideons came and passed out those maroon New Testaments. To actually feel that I had the Word of God and that I could hold it made such a great impression on me. That day I walked home feeling like I had a little piece of God in my hand.

Lowell

LOWELL was quite industrious and wanted to make some extra money, so he learned how to trap muskrats. Each morning on his way to school, he'd walk a couple of miles on the muskrat trap line. He did quite well and didn't like to see them get away. When one got out of the trap Lowell grabbed it with his bare hands. The muskrat bit him badly on the finger, but he hung on and put him away.

Lawrence Lundstrom

I was involved in muskrat trapping for the money. I used to trap muskrats with a neighbor,

Herbert Anderson, on shares. I would give him one-third for the privilege of trapping on his property. I worked hard because this was the only spending money I had.

Lowell

SOMEBODY had given Lowell a dog. It was a mix-breed and not suited to country life, so I gave it away to a family 10 or 12 miles away. But one morning the dog returned just after Lowell had hung all of his muskrat skins out to dry. The dog just demolished the whole lot of those muskrat furs, and Lowell felt awfully bad about that, but he wasn't remorseful for very long. He always had courage to go on again.

Lawrence Lundstrom

As a schoolboy I really needed to raise some extra money to buy school supplies and clothes. My parents didn't realize it, but I didn't have any sport shirts to wear to school except one of Dad's Hawaiian bowling shirts. I would have to roll the sleeves up to wear it, and I was kind of embarrassed about it, so I learned how to paint on glass and it was a craft that looked pretty good. Soon I found some buyers in the saloons of Peever. I also learned how to make little wooden characters and animals with a jigsaw. Those were my first business ventures.

Lowell

My parents were poor when I was a kid, but they did something for me that I'll always be thankful for. I know it was a real financial sacrifice. I was born with terribly crooked teeth. I had buck teeth "so bad I could eat corn through a chickenwire fence at 20 paces." My folks heard of a dentist in Minneapolis who could straighten teeth, and so they sent me to him.

Every two weeks I'd commute on the old Zephyr bus, 200 miles each way. Since I couldn't come more often than every two weeks, the dentist would tighten my teeth extra tight, and I would cry from the pain. It would seem to take forever to get from Minneapolis to Sisseton. I'm forever grateful, though, because millions of people see our smiles on TV, and someone recently said, "Those Lundstroms all have such beautiful teeth."

Lowell

God touched my life another time as a boy of 11 in a storefront revival meeting in Browns Valley, Minnesota. My cousin and I crept into the meeting hall one evening, and for some reason something in the service struck us both funny. We began to laugh, and before we knew it we had managed to disrupt the meeting. The man in charge of the service was so kind. He simply said, "Let's pray for these boys that God will touch their lives." As they prayed, we both got so under conviction that we literally crawled out of the service on our hands and knees.

Lowell

LOWELL was sort of impetuous, and one day he came home and out of the blue wanted me to teach him how to play the guitar. I knew a few chords, and so we sat down and I began a very brief instruction period.

Lawrence Lundstrom

I went to a one-room country schoolhouse. In a good year we'd have 13 kids in attendance and in a bad year we'd have maybe five. There was this girl in the eighth grade, a year ahead of me. One day, I got into an argument with her and she started telling all the things she could do. And I was dumb enough to start telling her all the things I could do. In a bragging contest of this kind, it's easy to get carried away. She told me she could do something and I said, "Why that's nothing. I can play the guitar." I shouldn't have told her that because it wasn't true. So she said, "You can play the guitar? I never heard you could play the guitar. Are you sure?" And I said, "Yup."

She said, "My folks are invited over to your folks' house this Saturday evening and I'm coming with them so I can hear you play the guitar." I said, "You're really coming, huh?"

Well, I got home early from school that day and saw my dad out in the barnyard. So I said, "Dad, teach me everything you know on the guitar." And he said, "What's the hurry?" I said, "It's time I learned some music."

I worked real hard and blistered my fingers on those strings, and by the end of the week I could sing and play, "Good Night, Irene." You talk about tension at Carnegie Hall, it was nothing to compare with what this country boy felt waiting for that girl to show up.

I would pace back and forth with guitar in hand, looking out the window, waiting for her to come. I would show her! My fingers were sore, but my heart was hot.

Eight o'clock came and no one showed up. Nine o'clock arrived, then 10 o'clock, and I was still looking. By 11 o'clock I finally realized that I'd been shot down again. Now isn't that just like a woman to blow a man's ego right down the tubes?

Shortly after World War II there were a lot of people drifting through Peever looking for a place to get situated, and quite a number of them were guitar players. They would hang out around the saloons, and so I began slipping into these places to watch the guitar players. I was picking it up pretty fast and most of them weren't willing to show me what they knew. They'd say, "Look out for that Lundstrom kid because he'll learn all you know." So I'd hide at the end of the bar and peek through the beer bottles until I saw where they'd position their fingers. Then I'd jump on my horse and ride home a mile away and practice what I'd learned.

Lowell

THERE was a boy from Illinois who came to visit his grandparents on a nearby farm. He played the trumpet, and he played it quite well. I remember he asked Lowell if he could play his guitar along with him. Well, the two of them played for some time, Lowell just standing there as though he were reading the notes. When they were finished with the song, the boy couldn't believe Lowell couldn't read a note of music. He was right on every note. He was always very good.

Lawrence Lundstrom

I heard about a talent contest in my home town of Peever. It was a little town that had only one square block of buildings in the business district. But they had a bunch of saloons. All the people gathered for the contest at the auditorium. I came in early with my dad's old guitar and set it down in the furnace room at the rear of the auditorium. Jealousy was so great in that little town that somebody got into my case and completely de-tuned the bottom three strings. Of course I didn't know it, and I got up to sing.

Lowell

I'LL never forget the sound that came out of that old guitar when Lowell hit the first chord. But he didn't quit. Instead, he played on the top three strings, sang loud and played low and still won the contest. He sang "Your Cheatin' Heart" and won the first prize of $8.

Lawrence Lundstrom

What a tremendous feeling of exhilaration, accomplishment and vindication I felt as I walked into the restaurant afterward and cashed that $8 check.

Lowell

2.

My Rock 'N Roll Days

MADGE and I decided to send Lowell to Morris Agriculture School. We'd changed farms, and I had a silo built in 1954, and on the silo I put "LUND-STROM & SONS" in hopes that my boys were going to farm with me. I'd hoped we'd have a big farm enterprise there, but we lost one boy not long after our move.

Lowell went to Morris Ag School which had a six-month term. That meant I had him as a worker for the other six months. Lowell worked hard through those summer months, and he was a big help. Pretty soon, at the age of 13 or maybe 14, he started his own orchestra.

Lawrence Lundstrom

LOWELL, Connie and my kid sister, Cynthia (we called her Skip), were all friends. There were about fifteen kids from school who chummed around. Lowell was just a rawboned farm boy at the time, a good kid. As I recall, there were about eight of them that Lowell pulled together to form his dance band. My kid sister, Skip, was one of them.

Jack Adams
Publisher, Sisseton Courier

I'VE known Lowell since he was a small lad who would come into my bank with his father. But I got acquainted with him when he was 14 or 15 and started talking about buying automobiles and band instruments. I suppose we financed half-a-dozen band instruments and half-a-dozen old cars for him before he went into the ministry.

Harold Torness
President, Roberts County National Bank

LOWELL would hitchhike home from Morris Ag School and then schedule dances for the weekend. He was only 14, but he would get his group together, pack the instruments into our car, and off they'd go to play a dance someplace. Of course they were getting popular. If they hadn't been going to school they could have scheduled a dance every night of the week—that's how popular they were.

Madge Lundstrom
Lowell's mother

I started my own little dance band when I was 13, almost 14. When I started getting bookings, Dad would come along. Things were kind of loose. If you had a band, you could just go right into saloons or dance halls and set up. Nobody ever bothered to ask our age. The first night I played I think we earned $6. I called the group Lowell's Rhythmairs.

I started playing those dances, and I was very determined to get ahead. We used to practice, practice, practice.

As our popularity grew, I started needing better musicians, but some of them were drunks. I remember I used to have to sober a man up to get him to play. I thought he would make it through the dance, but one night about half way through, he wet his trousers right on stage. I never did like alcohol, growing up during this period and seeing so many people drunk so much of the time.

Lowell

ONE time we had a delegation of about forty bankers in Sisseton for a meeting of the Clearing House Association, and it was our responsibility to provide dinner and a little entertainment for these fellows. Of course these gentlemen were country bankers from northeastern South Dakota. They were gray-haired, and quite a few of them were bank presidents who would rather discuss business than anything else.

We had asked Lowell Lundstrom to come and play for the group after the dinner. He brought a drum, a guitar and a few other things, and that night he was a one-man band. It was about the time Elvis Presley was making it big, and Lowell showed up in some fancy Western wear and blue suede shoes. Well, he put on a real show for those bankers, but I think a few of them left with hearing problems. Lowell had the amplifiers turned up pretty high, and some of the old gentlemen in the back had their ears covered up.

Harold Torness

So we played all these little places and began to break into some of the larger dance halls. Horace Height, the nationally known talent scout, came through Dakota country and held a contest. I entered and out of 99 contestants I won second prize.

A local fellow had a radio show and asked me to be on one of his programs. I soon became a regular on his show every Saturday on KWAT in Watertown. Not long after, he got a better job in another city and let me have his show. Soon I got on KDIO in Ortonville, Minnesota, and another little station up in that area.

All of a sudden, people were hearing a lot about us, so the places we played started to fill up. We were the first band in the whole area that had guitars instead of horns. We grabbed onto the rock 'n roll beat first, and when Elvis made his first hit record, "That's All Right, Mama," we learned it off the record. In just a few days we were performing it really well.

Lowell

WHILE Lowell was attending Morris Ag School and playing in the clubs and dance halls, he met a nice girl by the name of Connie Brown. She was his date one evening, and he was smitten with her. He would see her as often as he could, but with all the dances he had scheduled that wasn't very often. She didn't play in his band, so there wasn't any point in her going along.

Madge Lundstrom

I met her at a nightclub called The Ranch, located east of Sisseton. A friend was supposed to date Connie and I was to take the other girl; but I took one look at Connie, and I said, "You take the other one. I'm taking Connie." I started dating her, and we hit it right off. She was a pretty girl and she could dance well. She sang nice harmony with a good alto voice, and pretty soon I asked her to play in my band.

Lowell

CONNIE decided, with some persuasion from Lowell, to learn to play the guitar. I'll never forget when I went over to the Browns' and saw Connie practicing so hard. She was playing the music, trying to learn it, and her fingers were so tender.

Madge Lundstrom

I remember my first date with Lowell. I was supposed to be with another boy that evening, but Lowell sort of spirited me away from him and we ended up having a nice evening together. Lowell was so self-sure and seemed to know exactly what he wanted and how he was going to get there.

I'll never forget our second date. Lowell was a lot of fun to be around, but at an early age he was a serious young man. We were sitting in a booth at the nightclub, and Lowell turned to me and said, "If anything ever comes of our relationship, I want you to know two things—I will either be a country-Western entertainer or I will be a minister of the Gospel." He was only 14 at the time, and this almost floored me. I knew his background and knew he never went to church anywhere, yet one of the two things he felt he might be in life was a minister. I think that illustrates how prayers follow through the generations. Lowell had a godly grandmother who prayed constantly for the family.

Connie (Mrs. Lowell) Lundstrom

Connie learned to play the guitar and sing the songs, and pretty soon she was on stage with the rest of us. She was happy at first, but then she really got sour about it.

PHOENIX FIRST ASSEMBLY
13613 N. Cave Creek Rd.
Phoenix, AZ 85022

Because I was doing the rock 'n roll tunes of the day, many girls would respond by trying to catch my eye. They really thought I was something. Connie would stand behind me on stage and see all of this going on, and it really bothered her.

Another thing that bothered her was the fact that she was a backslider. She had once really known the Lord; and once you have a relationship like that, you can't find happiness in those smoke-filled clubs. All the drinking, fighting and immorality—it was a crummy life. But I thought it was great. I was making money, and I was getting ahead in the entertainment business.

The Grand Old Opry Show from Nashville, Tennessee, started making tours through our part of the country. I would have some of the stars as guests on my radio shows. I'll never forget the time Ferlin Husky came to Watertown, South Dakota, for a show. He had on a white suit, white hat and silver boots. He was a big star and a masterful entertainer. He and Carl Smith and Marty Robbins arrived in three Cadillac limousines—and to a country boy just starting out, that was something to behold.

Ferlin walked out on that stage to a roar of approval from the audience, and he entertained them for nearly two hours. As the audience clapped and whistled, I said to myself, "I'd give anything if I could just have what he has." Of course I had nothing, but that was beside the point at the time.

Well, time went by and about ten years later I had found the Lord and we were making a record in Minneapolis. We needed another guitar player to fill out the group; so when I read Ferlin Husky was in town at the Flame Club, I called Jimmy Colvard, Ferlin Husky's best guitar player, to see if he would play. Jimmy invited me over to talk about it and introduced me to Ferlin Husky.

I thought I might never get another chance again, so I gave him my testimony. After a few minutes he put his hands up and stopped me. He said, "Lowell, my daddy was a Baptist deacon and my mom was a Spirit-filled Christian." Then he looked at me very carefully and said, "Lowell, I'd give everything I've got if I could have burning inside me what's burning inside you."

Here was a man who had it all—fame, money, popularity—and yet he was empty inside. I've often marveled at the message of that incident.
Lowell

AFTER Lowell met Connie, they hit it off pretty well, and he'd keep seeing her when he was home on weekends from Agriculture School. Shortly after they started going together, Connie invited Lowell to attend church with her. Connie's sister, Ethel Hillberg, bought a New Testament and gave it to him and asked him to read it.
Madge Lundstrom

Connie's sister, Ethel, invited us to church because they were having some out-of-town musical evangelists for meetings. They played guitars, and in those days there weren't too many guitar players in church in South Dakota. I liked the Gospel music immediately. It had a unique quality that left something with you— not like the songs I was wailing in the dance halls and clubs. That was the first time it dawned on me that I might be able to play my guitar for the Lord.

Lowell

I invited Lowell to attend Easter Sunday services with me at the little Assembly of God church I attended. I was a little worried that he might think we were a little weird. The people there praised the Lord out loud, and I knew he wasn't used to that.

Connie Lundstrom

Then one Sunday Connie invited me to church. Before the preacher said half-a-dozen sentences, I knew someone had filled him in on me. He preached the Gospel so straight that I came under great conviction. God manifested His presence in that service through the gifts of the Spirit, and he discerned what I was saying in my heart while he was preaching.

I was so angry I stormed out of there and thought, "I will never go back again."

Lowell

LOWELL'S anger was of great concern to me. I hadn't yet recommitted my life to Christ, but I was miserable in those clubs and wanted us both to change. I really thought I had lost him as far as coming to church with me was concerned.

Connie Lundstrom

Many nights when I was running my dance band, before I met Connie, I would plan to go out after the dance and have a good time. I'd plan to get my buddy and some girls and live it up. Every night of wickedness I planned would never come to pass. The party would always fall through or break up early. My plans for evil would be ruined. I know now that God spared my life because He knew I would eventually be in His service. He didn't want any marks upon me for the ministry. He kept me by His grace even before I knew Him.

Lowell

LOWELL was doing quite well with his band. He was making lots of money, especially for a kid, and he was popular. I worried about him some though because he'd stay up so late on weekends and then get up early to go to school. I knew he was losing a lot of sleep.

Lawrence Lundstrom

I said I wouldn't, but I went back to that church with Connie. I didn't like what Pastor B.

C. Heinze was saying to me. Who was he to tell me to repent? I was a pretty good person in my own eyes. He really made me angry.

Connie and I were driving back from a dance one night. I wasn't going to give my life to Christ. I'd been thinking about it and had made up my mind.

I got so sleepy that I asked Connie to drive for me. We were pulling a trailer full of band instruments. Before dozing off, I reached into the glove compartment where I kept a schedule of engagements. I looked at the schedule and saw all the money I was going to make. As I was thinking about that, God spoke to my heart, "Lowell, what will it profit you if you gain the whole world but lose your soul?"

I saw what I was doing: I was selling my soul to gain the world. I wanted to make something out of Lowell Lundstrom. I didn't want to give up my dance band to follow Christ. I was under such heavy conviction that finally I just turned toward the door and said, "God, just leave me alone."

God left me alone, and I fell asleep, but the next thing I heard was Connie screaming at the top of her voice. I bolted upright as the car left the road and catapulted through the dark night. We were flying through midair. As I heard Connie screaming, I thought, "We're going to crash, and I'm going to die, and I've just told the Lord to get out of my life." I cried out, "O God, please give me another chance!"

The car hit the plowed field. The impact almost destroyed the car, the instruments and the trailer we were pulling. Miraculously we made it out of the crash alive. Connie had hit a patch of ice. The patrolman said he couldn't understand how that patch of ice had remained when the rest of the road was completely clear. I knew it was God's way of showing me how tragic it would be to die and lose my soul.

Lowell

YOU'D have thought Lowell would have given his heart to the Lord after such a close call, but he kept playing the dances, and I kept going with him. I really hated the environment but I was a part of his band and vocal group. We kept on going to church occasionally, and I know the Lord was working on Lowell not only there but in his heart.

Connie Lundstrom

One morning I was on my way to school. I was a senior. I had clothes, a new car, money, everything going my way. As I drove along I admired the beautiful car and said to myself, "Lundstrom, you're doing okay for yourself, aren't you?" Immediately God spoke to my heart once again, "Lowell, what will it profit you if you gain the whole world and lose your soul?" He had interrupted some pleasant thoughts with that convicting message, and again I said, "God, just leave me alone."

I had played a dance the night before and returned home around 3:30 a.m. I was on my way to school when I dozed off at the wheel. The next thing I heard was the grinding sound of metal on metal, and it seemed that all my sins flashed before my eyes in a split second. Instinctively I cried out, "O God, give me another chance!"

I realized I had sideswiped a huge truck. If I'd been another foot over I'd have been killed instantly.

I jumped out of the car and ran to the driver of the truck. He was in a daze. He said, "Kid, I don't know who was with you." I asked, "What do you mean?" He replied, "As soon as I saw your car on the horizon, something told me you were going to hit me, and I've been driving over here on the edge of the road where I could get away from you." I looked, and sure enough there were tracks in the gravel and grass where that big truck had been traveling.

That accident got my attention, and I began inquiring among Christians as to what serving the Lord was all about.

Lowell

3.

Wait Till Everybody Hears About This

LOWELL kept coming to church with me, especially after the second accident. He'd enjoy the music and squirm through the message. Sunday afternoons were very uncomfortable for both of us because we'd usually end up arguing. He felt the preacher was always preaching right at him, trying to get him to change his ways. We usually went to the movies on Sunday night, but one night Lowell said, "I feel like going to church instead."

Connie Lundstrom

I'd go to church on Sunday morning with Connie, and that preacher, the Reverend B. C. Heinze (thank God for that faithful man and his wife), would hit me right between the eyes with

the convicting message of repentance. I'd be under such conviction that I'd take the little Gideon New Testament I had received in the country school as a boy and check out what Reverend Heinze had said. The minister was always right and that would infuriate me.

I'd been to church with Connie one particular Sunday morning, and I was under conviction. I heard them announce a seven-thirty prayer meeting before the evening service at eight o'clock. I told Connie I felt like going that evening, so at seven-thirty sharp I was there; in fact, I was the only one on time. I learned later that the Christians usually arrived 15 minutes late. Anyway, I waited a few minutes, and when no one showed up for the prayer meeting I went upstairs to the main sanctuary. I was really steaming. I sat down by Connie and then I saw a crack in the door to the pastor's study. I figured he was in there getting ready to blast me again, so I went down and knocked on his door.

I went in and he said, "How are you doing?" I said, "Not very good at all. You've got this crazy idea that I have to repent to be born again, that I have to give up my dance band to be a Christian. I want you to know I'm as religious as anybody. I believe in God. I go to church and sing a hymn at the end of my radio broadcasts. I figure I'm about as religious as a man ought to be." Then he told me, "But Lowell, you need to give your heart to the Lord."

Lowell

I was at church the night Lowell gave his heart to the Lord. I could tell he was in the midst of a great internal struggle. He and Connie were sitting in the back row on the left side of the old church. That night when Lowell went forward and knelt at the altar, well I'll tell you, that was a time of great rejoicing.

Mrs. Clair Brooks
Gloria Lundstrom's mother and
Larry Lundstrom's mother-in-law

I sat there in church that Sunday night and knew the Lord wanted me to repent of my sins and follow Jesus. Part of my problem was I didn't want to follow anybody. I wanted to be the leader. It was part of my nature. There was a great struggle going on that night because it seemed like God was pulling me one way and the devil was pulling the other way. As I sat there I could feel the pulling and I wondered, "Should I go up there?"

The one great fear I had was, If I followed Jesus would I end up going back to my old life? I kept saying, "I'm not strong enough to change from what I've been doing." I didn't know God would do all that for me once I made the commitment.

Just about the time I was ready to give my life to Christ, something said, "Don't do it." I realized for the first time that this was the devil. I said, almost out loud, "Devil, leave me alone." Then I prayed, "Lord, I don't know if you can save a sinner like me," but I went forward and as I prayed I began to feel so clean. I felt like I had been scrubbed inside with Ivory soap. Then I noticed Connie praying beside me. When she looked up, I saw her smiling through her tears, a smile I never saw till then. She was happy to be back with Jesus.

Then I started to laugh. I was so happy. I rose from my knees and I said, "Wait till everybody hears about this!"

Lowell

LOWELL came home one day and announced to me that he really needed a player for his band. As his younger brother, I had a premonition of what was coming. I'd played in his band as a drummer until we had a squabble and I quit for a while. On this particular day his need seemed very urgent, and I was the only bass player available, so I agreed to help him. He already knew what my answer would be and had stopped on the way home and purchased a stand-up bass. He talked me into buying this antique for $375, and we continued playing dances. I'd make $5 a show and had paid it down to about $200.

Then one Sunday night I heard a ruckus in the kitchen and went downstairs to investigate. I heard doors slamming and my mother screaming, and finally I asked, "Lowell what in the world is going on?" He told me excitedly about his decision to follow Jesus and that he had decided to quit the dance band. I said, "That's a fine how-do-you-do. Here I sit high and dry with a debt of $200 and no job in sight."

Larry Lundstrom
Lowell's second-youngest brother

LOWELL came to me and said, "Mom, I want you to write letters canceling the remainder of dances on my schedule." If I remember correctly, he had about thirty-two dances scheduled at different places in South Dakota and Minnesota.

I tried to reason with him. He'd bought a new Rambler and I said, "Son, if you could just keep your schedule the way it is, in two or three months you could have your car paid for." I didn't really understand the experience of salvation and what Lowell had already understood the importance of: making a clean cut with the world. Lowell said, "Mom, don't make it any harder for me than it is."

Well, I wrote those letters for him, sealed them, stamped them and put them in a paper bag for him to post.

Madge Lundstrom

WHEN Lowell made the decision to cancel all those bookings, it was a big step. I remember I was both scared and excited at his decision. Once Lowell set his mind to a situation there was no stopping him. I remember watching the drama of the moment. For three days Lowell carried those letters in the brown paper bag in his car, mulling the whole chain of events in his mind. You could just feel the pull of the world and the pull of God on his life.

Connie Lundstrom

The day I decided to mail those letters the tension was high. I had been sitting in the car wondering whether I should mail them. Finally the pressure became so great that I knew I had to take action. I grabbed that bag of letters and headed for the post office entrance. I walked past several people and directly up to the window. I slammed that sack of mail down with some degree of force and declared in a firm, authoritative voice, "Mail them!" The mail clerk was completely taken aback. I'm certain he must have wondered why I found it necessary to be so dramatic over a sack of letters. What he didn't know was that he had just witnessed my second decision, spiritually.

Lowell

MOST of the dance hall managers accepted Lowell's cancellation letter, but there were a few who held us to our contract. In the meantime, Lowell was on me like a bird dog on a point with questions like, "Larry, if you died today would you make heaven your home? Would you really go to heaven today?"

Ever since he'd started acting strangely, that had

been one of the questions I'd tried to dodge. I couldn't say, "Yes," because there were things in my life that weren't right. I hadn't settled things with God. I didn't even go to church, but the Lord used Lowell's questions to prick my conscience. Those were questions I just couldn't shake.

Larry Lundstrom

Twenty-seven of the 32 dance hall managers accepted my cancellation letter. Five wouldn't let me off so easy, so I was bound by contract to fulfill those engagements the coming week. I wanted so badly to testify to my band members and to all those people. I had the desire to tell them of the love I had in my heart for Christ, but I didn't have the ability to communicate it. I was getting nowhere testifying. I wasn't being effective.

After the second dance, as I was driving home, tears came to my eyes and I said, "Lord I don't know what it is, but there has to be something more for me than what I've already received." I recalled that prayer for my pastor on the following Sunday, and he said, "Lowell, what you really need is the fullness of the Holy Spirit in your life." I said, "Pastor, what is it?" And he said, "Lowell, the Holy Spirit will give you power."

I figured that was what I needed, so he suggested that I attend the Monday evening fellowship meeting.

I didn't know what a fellowship meeting was, but I thought it might be a time when fellows got together. I went with the pastor, his wife, and evangelist Bonetta Rabe to this meeting in Watertown.

I remember I had this tremendous hunger, I needed God. That was all I could think of during the service. At the end of the service, the minister asked if anyone was interested in receiving the Holy Spirit. I immediately went forward and knelt in prayer. As I was praying, God deluged me with the tremendous outpouring of His power. It was so powerful that before I realized what was happening, I was praising God in words I had never spoken before. It was a powerful experience. I rushed home to tell my mom and dad about it.

Lowell

WE lived on a road close to Indian territory, and it was nothing unusual for somebody quite drunk to pound on the door, dance at the door, then talk to himself and go on his way.

On this particular night, a car drove up and the occupant sat in it for quite a spell before I heard the door slam. Next thing I knew, someone was mumbling at the front door, so I hollered, "Lawrence, I think there's a drunk Indian at the door." Lawrence went to the door, and Lowell burst through it.

Now, we're a close family but we're not the kind

of family that's gushy, kissing one another and things like that. Lowell grabbed his dad around the neck, gave him a kiss on the cheek and said, "I've seen Him, I've seen Him!" The way he acted was very alien to me, and I went upstairs straight to my room, and I told him, "Don't bother me with that. Stay away from me." He was trying to share an exciting experience with me; but not being a Christian at the time, I didn't understand it, didn't even want to. I know I hurt him in that way.

Madge Lundstrom

For some reason the light on the porch was out when I arrived at home, and I couldn't find my key. I banged on the door until Dad came down and let me in. The first words out of his mouth were, "Well son, what's happened to you? Your face is shining like a light bulb." I blurted out, "Dad, God saved me the other night, but tonight He filled me with His Holy Spirit." Dad was excited for me; but not being a Christian yet, he didn't know how to handle me, so he said, "Well, I think we'd better go upstairs and tell your mother."

There Mom was with the old family Bible, trying to find some way to get saved without giving her heart to the Lord. She was trying to pull it all together.

Well, the Spirit of the Lord poured out of me and scared my mom and dad so bad they said, "Son, you'd better go to bed now." The next

morning, my mom was so angry she said,
"Lowell, I'd rather see you dead than what's
happened to you."
Lowell

I didn't make it too easy on Lowell that morning,
either. I told him that all the people were talking,
that they thought he'd been running through the
pasture and hit his head on a rock. I was still angry
about being left high and dry with a bass I wouldn't
be able to use anymore after the next five dances.

After the second dance, I had given my heart to
the Lord and Lowell had just received the Holy
Spirit. After the third dance, with Lowell and me
witnessing to the rest of the people in the band,
they refused to ride with us anymore. They
couldn't stand the conviction our changed lives
and testimony brought on them. They were losing
money by having to drive their own car to the
dances.

Suddenly, there was tremendous power in
Lowell's words. He'd stand out there in those
dance halls and clubs and give his testimony. Then
he'd turn around to those of us in the band who
were Christians and say, "Praise God, we will
never have to play that dirty song in this place
again." I remember him saying after the last commitment, "Hallelujah, we're finished!" My brother
was headed in a new direction just as hard if not
harder than any he had ever pursued.

Larry Lundstrom

I was in the living room of the Lundstrom home a few nights after Lowell had received the Holy Spirit. I remember his dad was full of questions. He just kept asking Lowell one question after the other, and I knew Lowell had no training in how to answer them. He knew nothing about the Scriptures; and yet, miraculously, he'd turn in the Bible and there the answers would be for the specific questions. I kept praising God inside because the Holy Spirit was guiding him to the answers to his father's questions.

Connie Lundstrom

4.

A Break with the Past—
A New Beginning

It was spring when I fulfilled my last dance commitment, and I needed work. I found a job with an unbelieving farmer who was a member of a dead, ritualistic church. He gave me the job of clearing rocks off the top of fields.

In northeastern South Dakota the ground is rocky, and the spring thaws seem to push the rocks up out of the ground. I wasn't used to manual labor and the going was really rough. The farmer would sense this and taunt me with questions like, "Wasn't the dance band easier than this?"

As the days went by, I saw him get more and more under conviction. He would get violent and begin to curse as we worked. He'd be on one end of a piece of farm equipment cursing, and I'd be on the other end praising God to counterbalance the bad language.

I gave him a hard day's work for the $6 a day he paid, but one day he threw down his wrench and said, "You're fired!" I looked him straight in the eye and said, "The only reason you're firing me is because you can see Jesus in my life and you can't stand the guilt." I got into the car and headed for town. I pulled into Les Stillson's Phillips 66 station and got out of the car.

Lowell

I'D known Lowell since he was a kid. I'd see him in town when his dad and mom would stop by for gasoline. When he had his dance band and radio program, I was one of his program sponsors. I remember he was only supposed to talk about us for 30 seconds, but Lowell would get excited about our service station and he'd talk for a minute and a-half or longer.

One day in the spring he drove into my station and said, "Les, I need a job." I laughed and said, "What are you talking about? You've got more than you can handle." Lowell said, "I've made a big decision. I've given my heart to the Lord and I want to serve Him. I'm going to Bible school in the fall, but I've quit my dance band and I need a job until school starts."

We agreed on wages and I gave him a job. He was a good worker, and he visited with the customers. He was a good salesman, too. One day I said, "Lowell, we've got a whole bunch of polish here. I bought some Hart's Auto Polish; it's good polish, but it doesn't sell well off the shelf. I've got six or seven cases here and it's just not moving."

He said, "Les, you know I'm not going to sell anything that's not any good." I said, "It is good; here, I'll show you." We went out back where there was a faded old car and I showed him.

After that, whenever someone would pull into that drive for gasoline Lowell would treat them to a demonstration. He'd have a bottle of Hart's in one hand and a rag in the other, and while the gas was running he'd demonstrate it right in the middle of their hood.

He'd say, "See, you do need some of this Hart's Auto Polish." I always figured that somebody was going to get out and whip him one because he'd put a nice-and-shiny spot right in the middle of their hood. But Lowell sold every bottle of that polish and was looking for more, and I said, "Well no, Lowell, that's fine. We're not going to order any more Hart's Auto Polish."

Lowell was always a tremendous salesman and of course now he's in the biggest selling job there is—selling the work of the Lord.

Les Stillson
Owner, Stillson's Phillips 66 service station

LOWELL had proposed to Connie before they were both converted, and they made plans for a June wedding before going off in the fall to Bible school. It had always been a prayer of mine and my husband, Bud, that we would have a daughter who

Lowell
at age three.

Lawrence and Madge Lundstrom, who farm near Sisseton
(Lowell, Larry and Leon's mom and dad)

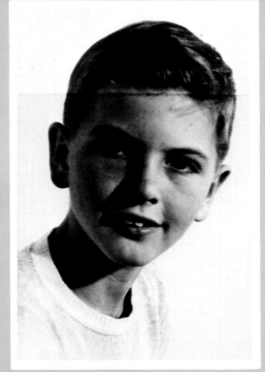

Even as a young lad, Lowell was industrious. He ran muskrat traps, painted designs on glass and made wooden decorative cut-outs to earn money for his school clothes.

Here's Lowell at 13, at the time he appeared on the Horace Heidt Talent Contest.

Lowell and
Connie dating

The Dance Band days begin.

Lowell's dance band was one of the first to play rock'n roll music in South Dakota and people flocked to night clubs to hear them perform. Pictured here is his group known as the Rhythmairs.

It was only a few months after Lowell was converted that he and Connie were married. They were wed June 14, 1957 before going to Bible College in the fall.

Lowell didn't wait long to begin the ministry after he was converted. Though some of his teachers at Bible College felt he needed more training, Lowell launched out enthusiastically and God blessed his efforts richly. This photo was taken the evening of his first sermon.

Wedding day,
June 14, 1957

Connie and Lowell with their little Rambler. It served them well during the early days of their ministry.

This photo was taken shortly after Lowell and Connie went to Bible School in Devil's Lake, North Dakota. During their time there, they would minister whenever and wherever opportunities were available.

Lowell and Connie begin as a young couple in the ministry.

Rev. Ray Rushing was the man who gave Lowell $60
to begin a radio program.

During the early years, the ministry team consisted of Lowell,
Connie and Larry. Gloria joined them in 1965 after
she and Larry were married.

Larry joins
Lowell and Connie in
the summer of '61.

Lou Giroux was steel guitarist later on in '61.

The cars transported us during the early days.

In 1965 the Lundstroms acquired this 20-year-old Flexible bus. It looked pretty good until they tried to drive it. Pictured in the inset is Larry whose ministry duties included keeping the old bus going. According to Gloria, Larry spent much more time under it than in it.

Larry marries Gloria, and she becomes a great part
of the musical family.

Londa and Lisa,
Lowell and Connie's
daughters, as they
appeared in 1966.

Happiness is a bus that runs. Londa and Lisa got plenty of playtime outside whenever the bus broke down...and that was often. They always tried to be a big help whenever possible.

Later on,
Londa
begins
to sing.

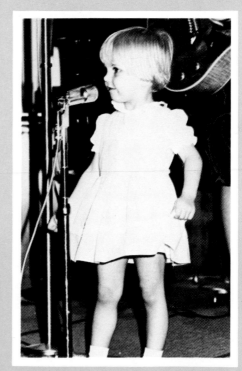

Lisa always
received
a big
response!

When Lowell Jr. was born, Dad had a way of studying
and babysitting at the same time.

The old bus often "gave up the ghost"!

Digging out of a mud hole at Trossacks Bible Camp near Wyburn, Saskatchewan, Canada.

Steve Booher joins the Lundstroms as pianist.

The day they pulled up to the Custom Coach Company to pick up their new bus was a happy day for the Lundstroms. Eight months earlier it looked like sheer impossibility but God provided the funds—$72,000, to make this miracle. Today the Lundstroms' 18-member ministry team travels in two such well-equipped coaches.

The children have really grown since this
day at Mount Rushmore.

Madge Lundstrom coverted her porch into an office to keep pace with Lowell's growing ministry. She remains active in the management of the headquarters in Sisseton.

Lowell, Londa, LaShawn (Larry and Gloria's daughter) and Lisa working on a song.

Tent crusades
were part of
the ministry.

Paul Secord, pianist, and his wife, Mahala, traveled with the Lundstroms for two years.

Londa becomes pianist at 10. Bill Simmons, guitarist, and Leon (Lowell's brother who plays drums) have already been part of the band.

Mack Thomas, on top left, was steel guitarist for a year.

The children
are growing.

Listening to
Bible stories
in the bus

The Lundstroms begin to mature as a family and
a ministry musical group.

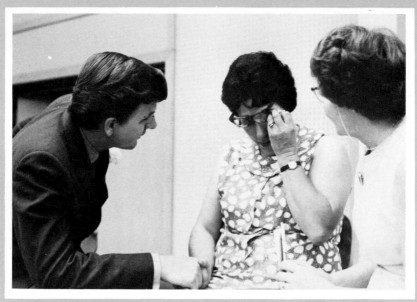

Personal concern has always marked Lowell's ministry.

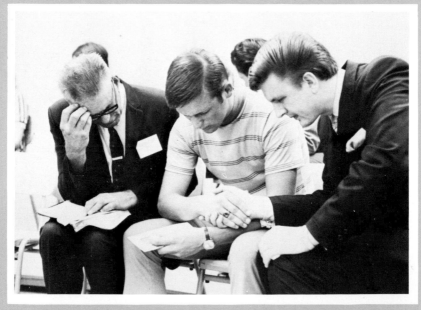

He spends time with people after every rally to help them meet Christ in a new and exciting way.

The Lundstroms—1979!

A recent photo with "little Lance," age 1 year.

Huge crowds come to see and hear the Lundstroms wherever they go. Through the Lundstroms' singing and Lowell's powerful messages, more than 15,000 persons are converted in rallies and crusades each year.

Lowell
calling people
to Christ.

The holy scene
of seekers dedic-
ating their lives
to Christ inspired
Lowell and the
family to live
on the highway
for more than
two decades.

would be part of a ministry for Christ. As Connie and Lowell were preparing for marriage and the ministry, it was like a dream come true; it was a real answer to prayer.

Alice Brown
Connie's mother

THEY had a beautiful wedding. It was very simple. They didn't have too much money and neither did we or Connie's parents. They had a lot of friends in Sisseton who had flowers growing in their yard. They'd call on these friends and ask if they could have some of their flowers for the wedding. The people were very gracious.

Instead of the bridesmaids having special dresses, they all wore their graduation gown, and the mixed colors with all those flowers was really something to see. Lowell composed and wrote a wedding song to Connie. The church was full. Lowell sang his new song to Connie and she sang to him. It was really touching.

Connie was thrifty. She borrowed her cousin's wedding gown, and Lowell got himself a white jacket. It wasn't fancy, but the people really appreciated the beauty of it and enjoyed the wedding very much.

Madge Lundstrom

I remember that on the night of their wedding Lowell was pretty excited. While he was waiting for the ceremony to begin, he decided to brush his teeth one more time. In the rush of things, he grabbed a tube of Brylcreme hairdressing instead of toothpaste. He brushed his teeth for several seconds before he realized what he had done and by then it was too late.

Alice Brown

WE would always take good care of Lowell when he came into the bank. He always had great aspirations and plans and expected at that time to become one of the famous fellows like Lawrence Welk, produced out here on the Dakota plains. Lowell's dreams were such that it was awfully hard to turn him off when he started talking about his plans.

It was quite a surprise to me when Lowell came in one day and asked if we could extend some credit for him to go to Bible school. He said he had a young lady that appealed to him very much and didn't want to have him chasing around to dances, and we found ourselves extending some credit for his schooling.

Harold Torness

A lot happened to Connie and me in a short time. We'd found the Lord on April 7, 1957, were married on June 14, and entered Bible school in October of that same year. Connie and I went to Bible school up in Devil's Lake, North Dakota, at Lakewood Park Bible School. There we learned the Scriptures, sitting side-by-side. It was a small school with about fifty students.

We felt impressed to travel on weekends, holding services and giving our testimony and singing. Many of the teachers thought we might get hurt or be less than effective because of our lack of training, but the Lord really blessed our sincerity and our efforts. That was the beginning of our full-time ministry. We'd hold three services a week, and we did that for the entire three years we were there.

Lowell

DAD and I went up for Lowell and Connie's graduation in Devil's Lake. Connie was Valedictorian, and Lowell was Salutatorian. Dad and I had been converted before Lowell and Connie left for Bible school, and their graduation was of great significance to us as Christians.

They decided Lowell should attend North Central Bible College in Minneapolis, so in the fall of 1960 he enrolled. Connie didn't attend that fourth year. She went to work full-time so they could be self-sufficient, and they still had their full-time ministry.

Madge Lundstrom

Professors like John Phillips and Ray LeVang were a real influence on me. Those men gave me a feel for the Bible that I'd never known before. They also gave me a tougher view of the world

**around me. This led me to understand how I
might better present the Gospel to the secular
mind.**

Lowell

I lived in an apartment with four other fellows.
Lowell and Connie lived next door. To be honest,
the walls were pretty thin and there wasn't much
privacy. When Lowell and Connie would practice
their music, it was as though they were in the room
with us. They had a radio broadcast even then, and
when they'd set their tape recorder on the table to
tape their broadcast we could hear every word.

Let me tell you, Lowell was an inspiration to all of
us. I can remember very few weekends that didn't
start with the Lundstroms packing up their weath-
ered Nash Rambler wagon in preparation to minister in some distant church. I can remember more
than a few Monday mornings when he and Connie
would just be pulling into the school at a time when
the rest of us were just getting up to go to class. He
had a lot of determination then, and it's obvious
that it is a quality he's retained.

Jack Strom
*Former classmate and director of college
relations, North Central Bible College*

LOWELL was a real nut for Pepsi Cola. He just
loved the stuff. I recall one day when he opened a
bottle of Pepsi and it was as flat as a bad joke. That
didn't sit too well with Lowell, so he called the bot-

tler to complain. That afternoon they brought out a
full case of Pepsi for him. That Lundstrom, he always had a way of getting things done.

Craig Carter
Former classmate and pastor, Rochester,
Minnesota, Assembly of God

LOWELL came to us after being a dance band
leader in South Dakota. I felt back then that he was
rather naive, somewhat amazed by the harshness
of the world around him, considering his experience as a band leader. But I was taken by his open-
ness to confess his shock at some of the things
being discussed in the class. I appreciated his tal-
ents. It was obvious even then that he had the necessary tools to achieve the status he has. The only
question was whether he had the drive and dedication, and I guess he's answered that question.

John Phillips
Professor, North Central Bible College

5.

The Early Years

I have always marveled at Dad Lundstrom and how he had given up Larry, and later Leon, to be a part of Lowell's ministry when he needed them on his farm. But I think he's happy the Lord saw fit to pull them out of his farm operation and put them into the harvest fields for the Lord.

I remember when Connie and Lowell had their little Nash Rambler, going from place to place and singing and ministering. We'd marvel at the way (even in the beginning) Lowell could get up with just his little New Testament and no sermon notes and preach powerful messages. The Lord really did anoint him. That was what kept him going.

Carl Johnson
Longtime friend and secretary/treasurer of
Message for America

MY mom and dad were converted in one of Lowell's meetings. They were both in show business and played the nightclub circuit. One day they saw an ad in Winnipeg, and it had a picture of Lowell with a Gretch guitar.

My dad said, "Let's go out there tonight and see if that guy can play that thing." After the service, they invited Lowell and Connie over to the house. They didn't accept Christ right then, but Lowell and Connie would write them and say, "Rick and Lil, we want you to know we love you and we're praying for you."

About a year later my folks had a gig on Saturday night and afterwards drove down to Fargo, North Dakota, for the Lundstrom's Sunday rally. They accepted Christ into their lives that very day. I've often wondered what would have happened to them but for Lowell and Connie's deep interest and prayers for their salvation.

Bill Simmons
Musician for the Lundstroms

WHEN Lowell got through Bible school, he started scheduling services all over Colorado. He and Connie were still driving that Rambler Lowell had bought in high school, and the tires were so bad you could almost see the innertube. Lowell prayed about it in the service one night. After the service, he stepped outside the church, and up walked a man who hadn't even been in the service. He said, "Are you needing some tires?" Lowell replied,

"Yeah, where can I get some tires for my old Rambler?" and the man said, "Follow me."

Lowell and Connie followed the man to his home expecting to get some good used tires. The man went to the granary and pulled out two brand new tires and gave them to Lowell.

Madge Lundstrom

Larry graduated from high school about the same time I finished Bible school. Connie and I both played the guitar, and we felt that the addition of a bass would enhance our musical sound. Larry agreed to join us, and a few days later we departed for our next meeting. It was in Mondovi, Wisconsin, and it was a longer drive than we anticipated.

It was a very hot day and Larry had a huge boil on his leg. He was really miserable. That, combined with the tension, really took its toll on him.

We arrived 30 minutes late and had to hurriedly set up our equipment. The church was steaming hot inside. As we prepared to sing our first song, I looked over to check on Larry. His eyes were rolled back, he was leaning against the wall, and I realized he was fainting dead away. He fainted and fell off the stage before I could get over to him. He had a habit of fainting, my big, six-foot-three-inch younger brother. He fainted the day the vet gave his horse an injection, and he fainted in the dentist's chair.

They dragged him outside and revived him,

and in a few minutes he was all right. He got back up and played his bass the rest of the evening.

Lowell

AFTER Larry joined the group, the little Rambler station wagon just wouldn't hold all the equipment, so Lowell bought a small trailer somewhere. Pretty soon they outgrew that, so they purchased a small house trailer. It was more of an office; in fact, Lowell started printing a little newsletter on an old mimeograph machine. The mobile office was treacherous to drive because it would whip the car all over the road. One day while Madge and I were following them, that trailer was weaving back and forth so bad that Madge prayed out loud, "O Lord, if they'll just sell that thing, I'll help them with the office work in my house." I guess that was the beginning of the ministry headquarters.

Lawrence Lundstrom

AT first we drove our little Rambler and pulled a trailer, but as the team grew we really needed something larger. Larry and Gloria had gotten married, and she had joined the ministry team. We had so much equipment that we decided we needed a bus. We looked for a long time, but Lowell and Larry couldn't find anything we could afford. We were in northern California between meetings and spotted an old bus. It had been used as a disaster bus by the state of California. It had been equipped with typewriters, telephones and other equipment so they could report disasters. We purchased the disaster.

Connie Lundstrom

IT became our disaster. Before every trip Larry would spend the night under it. We'd drive it to a rally and invariably it wouldn't start. Larry would get some men from the church, and they'd be working on it till all hours of the night. I think Larry spent more time underneath it than in it. I almost thought Larry was married to that bus rather than to me.

Gloria Lundstrom
Larry's wife

We were on our way home from Oregon, and Larry was driving the old bus. Larry always had a habit, when driving the tractor at home, of turning the switch off and coasting downhill. On our way home from Oregon, we were going down some steep mountain roads and Larry decided he'd save some fuel, so he turned off the motor. The bus had an air compressor to power the air brakes, so when Larry turned off the engine the air compressor quit running and couldn't replenish the air necessary to stop the bus. He kept using the brakes when he came to each corner.

I was in the back of the bus, asleep. I kept

hearing this Sssssst! Sssssst! sound, but I couldn't hear the engine. Then all of a sudden I realized what Larry was doing. I jumped up and ran to the front of the bus. It had barely enough air to make one more brake. By pulling the emergency hand brake, we finally stopped the bus. I explained to Larry that he could have killed all of us, shooting right off the edge of the cliff on that Oregon mountain. He wasn't even aware of the crisis, but God had awakened me.

Lowell

We would hold meetings in churches across the country, and we were always pleased when we came across an energetic pastor. We had been invited to Marion, Indiana, to participate in a tent revival. The Reverend A. W. Thomason was the pastor and he was really enthusiastic! He was a fellow that liked to get things done.

We were to be there for five weeks, and both of us wanted to see the tent filled each night. Pastor Thomason had his own printing press at the church, which impressed me, and he could crank out literally thousands of handbills within a few hours.

One of us came up with what seemed to be a 24-carat idea. We would print thousands of fliers about the meeting and then drop them out of an airplane. For two or three days prior to the air drop, we were in neighborhoods with a loud-speaker on top of a car. We told the kids that we would have some special information for them and that it would come from the sky.

We found out a few hours before the drop, though, that the town had a ruling that prohibited airplanes from flying lower than 3,000 feet over the city. The ruling made us fly a lot higher than we had anticipated, but we made the drop anyway. Those days nobody equated scattered leaflets with pollution.

We didn't know the wind was about to shift. With great anticipation the pilot reached the legal altitude and A. W. gave the signal. Out went the fliers and all of a sudden it was like a white cloud as thousands of fliers came billowing out of the plane. Instead of going straight down, though, the fliers were blown several miles east of the city, missing it entirely but totally covering a trailer park. Some of the mobile homes were plastered with hundreds of leaflets. My Christian vocabulary will not allow me to fully describe the magnitude of that park owner's wrath.

Lowell

LOWELL, Connie and Larry were conducting a church meeting in Paynesville, Minnesota, about ninety miles from Sisseton. Both Lowell and Larry were sick with bronchial pneumonia, but they were determined to complete the meeting. Lowell did his best and even preached one or two nights sitting on a chair instead of standing.

They spent a couple of days in the hospital, but they weren't getting any better so they decided they'd be better off at our place. Dad and I would wait on them and try to keep them from getting up. Larry was really ill and losing ground. He had a high temperature and couldn't seem to stop coughing.

A neighbor man would faithfully stop by every morning and pray for them both, but one day Larry was at a real low point. Lowell became aware of that even though he was downstairs in another part of the house. In his weakened condition, he crawled up the stairs and gathered everybody around Larry's bed and said, "People, let's pray." I'll tell you, we really touched God that day. Lowell, sick as he was, led out in prayer.

From that very hour Larry started getting better. Both Lowell and Larry were weak for quite a spell, but they resumed their schedule soon afterward. Only God's protecting hand upon them kept them going.

Madge Lundstrom

OUT on the farm, hunting was a way of life and I taught all three of my boys to hunt. They really enjoyed it, and when Lowell and Larry would have a break between meetings in the late fall, they'd come home and we'd all go out shooting those big, northern ducks.

We would wait until the weather was real bad so those ducks would be flying low. Then we'd take the tractor and a high wagon box for shelter. One time we decided the weather was too rough for us. The snow was really coming down, and there was a danger of freezing.

When we went to start the tractor, I pushed the button and nothing happened. I'd forgotten to bring the crank, so we were stranded in an area too rough for a pickup or car and nobody knew how to find us.

Lowell looked at me and said, "Dad, let's pray." So we lifted our hands, and we prayed. When we finished, I went over and touched the starter and the engine fired up. We got out of there and made it home safely.

The whole week after, I kept going to that old tractor to see if I could make it start again without the crank but nothing would happen. It was only a miracle of the Lord.

Lawrence Lundstrom

LOWELL never carries any money. If it weren't necessary for the ministry, I doubt if he'd even think about it all. The ministry team was in Seattle for a crusade and Lowell, Larry, Connie and Gloria were staying with one of my sons. Lowell decided to make a trip downtown to a radio station and asked Larry to drive.

Seattle is separated by water, and there are several ferry crossings. As Larry pulled into the toll gate, he suddenly realized he had brought no money and asked Lowell for some help. Larry dug up

26¢, but Lowell didn't have a penny, so Larry asked the tolltaker, "Will you take 26¢ and let us cross?" The guy replied, "Sorry, mister, you'll have to turn around and go back." They had to drive half-way across town to get their wallets before they could go to the radio station.

Mrs. Brooks

LOWELL always had a way with finances. He would have so many projects going that we would leave on tour without any money at all out on the road. It set up a pattern in the first few years of our ministry. I somehow got the task of handling the books, and Lowell would come to me for money because we'd always have revenue from record sales. He would often send his money back to the office to meet some critical need.

After a few times of being in a tight spot, I devised a plan to help keep us somewhat solvent. He would come up and ask what had come in from the record sales, and I would hand him the cash box. Of course I would have removed $50 or $60 first and put it away for safe keeping. I'd let it build up to $1000, and inevitably some crunch would come along. Here would come Lowell wanting to know what came in from record sales. He'd say, "Is that it?" and I'd smile and push the cash box to him.

One day we had a real emergency, and Lowell came for the record receipts, counted them and shook his head. About fifteen minutes later, I dipped into the reserve and walked over to him and said, "Here's another $100 I found." About thirty minutes later I'd do the same thing, "Here's another $200 I found, Lowell," until I came up with the exact amount he was needing to send back to the office.

He used to wrestle with that, his kid brother holding out on him like that, but when I gave it all back to relieve the financial crunch he was sure thankful that I'd stored a little away for a rainy day.

Larry Lundstrom

As we traveled across the country, preaching and singing, we would meet thousands of people; and many of them really tried to go an extra mile to help us and make us feel welcome.

We were holding a meeting in El Centro, California, one time, and it was a great spiritual time for all of us. The Lord was really coming to our ministry in a tremendous way. We were having a great revival and it seemed to be a turning point in my ministry.

A doctor who attended the meeting inquired if we had had all of our immunizations. He wanted to donate a set of shots to us. I told him we hadn't been immunized and we would come in to see him in the next few days.

The weather was blistering hot in El Centro, and Connie and I slept in a minimum of clothes. One morning, very early, the door burst open; and I was half asleep, but I could see this guy with a hypodermic needle in his hand. I must have misjudged the distance between us because, before I could react, the doctor pulled back the covers and jammed the needle into our buttocks—he immunized us both right then and there.

Lowell

I had just joined the ministry team with my two brothers, Lowell and Larry, and among other things they had assigned me the responsibility of making sure we had offering containers on the bus. I was new to the routine of preparing for a meeting, and with all the rush I forgot to bring the containers. We used Kentucky Fried Chicken buckets because they were inexpensive and we could stack them in a small place.

We arrived for the meeting in eastern Tennessee, and as usual we were on a tight time schedule. About five minutes before the service was to start, I discovered my mistake and asked a Christian man from the audience to help me out. I said, "Would you go down to Colonel Sanders and get us 32 empty buckets? I need them right away for tonight's service." He looked at me kinda funny but nodded that he understood and left. After about an hour, the fellow showed up backstage with two buckets overflowing with fried chicken. He'd ordered two buckets with 32 pieces each.

Leon Lundstrom
Lowell's youngest brother

6.

Happiness is a New Bus

BEFORE the Lord provided us with the new buses, we drove an old 1946 Flexible, the kind that had no bathroom or air-conditioning. Our bathroom for the little children was empty ice cream buckets with lids. They didn't know what came in the ice cream buckets; they just knew that was their potty. Someone had given us 25 buckets, and the children would use them and then we would discard them.

A kind lady came to the bus one night with a grocery sack full of goodies for the team. In it were two buckets of ice cream. She'd also popped some popcorn and filled one of the buckets.

The lady came up to my 3-year-old daughter, LaDawn, and said, "Hi honey, look what I've brought you." LaDawn smiled and said, "Oh

goody, more new honey buckets to potty in."
Gloria Lundstrom

OUR old bus was in such poor repair that, in the winter, snow would drift in between the cracks and actually pile up during the night. It was so cold that we would dress our little ones in snow suits and snow boots and tuck them into warm sleeping bags. People saw us come into town in that bus and imagined we were on a continual vacation. Little did they realize what kind of an existence we endured.
Connie Lundstrom

That old wreck of a bus taught us patience. It didn't have any restroom facilities. The children were just tiny and they would have to get up in the middle of the night to use the "honey bucket." Instead of putting it away, they would often leave it right in the middle of the aisle. Many mornings I would step out of bed and hit the rim of that honey bucket. The fluid contents would flip onto my leg, and I can tell you it was a humbling experience.
Lowell

When we purchased the old Flexible I asked the man to give us an extra motor in case the old one stopped. He agreed and we propped the heavy thing up on blocks in the back of the bus.

I had to make a quick exit off the road one day, and the props slipped. The motor came crashing to the floor and landed just inches from where little 2-year-old Londa was sleeping. My, how good God was to protect us!

Lowell

WHEN they fire up those bus engines, the children of the team members are ready to go! They have one ear trained in that direction, and you don't even have to call. They're already inside the bus.

Mrs. Brooks

WE were conducting one-night rallies in the Eastern states. We were traveling on the Pennsylvania Turnpike and everyone was hungry, so we stopped at a cafe. We had a good dinner, and when Larry (our treasurer on the road) reached for his wallet he discovered he had left it in the bus. He turned to the waitress and said, "I'm sorry, but we don't have any money."

Sensing that she had somewhat of a problem on her hands she asked, "How are you going to pay for all of this?" Larry replied, "Well, I guess I'll just have to leave my wife." Larry is such a character that she almost believed him, but he told her he was only kidding and that he had forgotten his wallet on the bus. He said, "I'll just leave my wife here while I go after the money so you won't think I'll run off without paying."

We all got up to go, and I said, "Larry, I'm going to the powder room so wait for me. Don't forget me." So he paid the bill and walked out to the bus. While I was in there I had the funniest feeling that I had been left behind, and when I went to the door of the cafe the bus was gone.

As I was standing there, flustered, the waitress came up and said, "Aha, he really did mean it, didn't he!" I was stranded on the turnpike. A young boy drove up and seeing that I was upset asked, "What's the matter, lady?"

I told him I had missed the bus and he said, "Don't worry, there'll be another one along in about two hours." I said, "No, no, no, you don't understand; my husband was driving the bus, and he forgot me." The boy asked me where I was going, and I said, "I don't know." Then he asked me where I'd come from and I said, "I don't know that either." He said, "Lady, you really do need help! Hop in."

So away we went, chasing the bus. We finally caught up about ten miles down the road and flagged it over. They hadn't even missed me. The next week we left someone behind four different times. After that we decided we had better start taking roll call before departing.

Gloria Lundstrom

Steve Booher had joined the team to play piano for us and he was intrigued by the old bus. Never having driven one, he wanted to try his hand at it. Driving the bus is a job nobody likes, so we were more than happy to teach him how to drive it. The bus had rather poor brakes, and we were always careful to start slowing it a mile before we planned to stop.

We were on one of the Oklahoma turnpikes and Steve was driving. All of a sudden, I looked up and saw the toll booth ahead of us. Steve was unaware of the crisis at hand. He didn't know how bad the brakes were. He was going to crash through the toll booth at 50 miles per hour! Larry saw the crisis too.

We both jumped up and ran to the front. Larry slammed his foot down on top of Steve's on the brake pedal, and I grabbed the emergency brake. Cars were lined up at the booth and we knew what might happen if we hit them. We roared up to the line of cars. The bus was slowing but we wondered if it would stop in time. God's hand of protection was on us that day. We stopped less than six feet away from the car in front of us. If God hadn't awakened me when He did, the poor brakes on the old bus would have destroyed a lot of lives.

Lowell

Sometime after our close call with the toll booth, we were driving in North Dakota. Our bus was on its last leg when we happened to drive through Pembina where they make the big Greyhounds. As we drove through the town we came upon the bus factory, and out in front was this beautiful new Scenicruiser. We stopped and looked it over. It was exactly what we needed, but we were flat broke. We didn't have enough money to buy bird seed for a cuckoo clock. As I stood by the new bus, an assurance grew in my heart that the Lord would give us one like it. I laid hands on that bus and I said, "Lord, you know this bus costs $72,000 and I don't have the money, but I want you to give us this bus for the ministry."

God gave me an idea how to raise the funds for it. He told me, "Lowell, park the old bus behind the new one. Then take a photograph of them. Send one to your friends and ask them to help you. Then make a tour of all the churches that support you. Lowell, it is going to work."

Eight months later we went to the Custom Coach factory in Columbus, Ohio, and picked up a bus that was custom-built for the Lundstroms, and the bus was paid for in full, $72,000. I sat down at the wheel of that new bus and hit that loud air horn and shouted, "Hallelujah! Praise God for His goodness!"

Lowell

WE had spent an entire year on the road in crusades and one-night rallies. Every night Lowell would be up there singing and preaching. At the end of the December tour one year, we returned home to Sisseton and Lowell's voice was completely gone. He tried to sing Christmas carols on the bus with the kids on the way home but his voice just wouldn't respond.

Connie Lundstrom

We were listening to Glen Campbell, Mac Davis, the Carpenters, Andy Williams and all the others sing carols on this special Christmas radio program. I thought, "Lord, here I am 35 years old and I am already bombed out." I really think that had to be one of the saddest moments of my life.

The Lord sent us Chris Ward as the teacher for our children, but she was also a trained singer. Chris taught me vocal exercises and showed me how to sing from my diaphragm and use my stomach muscles better to support my singing. She came just at the right time. We still keep that rigorous schedule of crusades and one-nighters, but praise God, my voice is now as strong and clear as can be.

Lowell

7.

A Message for America

We were at a youth camp in Mitchell, South Dakota, and a Baptist minister heard us singing and preaching the Gospel. He was impressed with the message he heard and said, "Lowell, you preach the Gospel of salvation so straight you ought to be on radio." I said, "That's fine, but that costs money," and he replied, "I want to help you." He told me he was going to put me on a radio station.

I went to the little cabin in which we were staying and got down on my knees. I said, "Lord, here is a man who wants to put us on the radio. What should I call the program?" The Lord spoke to my heart, "Call it the Message for America." That was how our radio ministry began.

The minister took me to the radio station, and we discussed the cost. The station representative told us each broadcast would cost $6, so the man wrote out a check. I said I would like to be on the following week as well, so the minister gave me $30 and said, "Now sink or swim."

We started asking friends to help us stay on the station, and not long afterward we went on KXEL, a 50,000-watt station in Waterloo, Iowa. Little did I realize at the time that this would be the start of what is now a network of 150 stations across the U.S. and Canada carrying the Lundstroms' weekly radio program.

Lowell

THE Lord blessed our ministry those early years when we were holding revivals in churches; in fact, we continued to travel and preach in churches for the first 10 years of our ministry. We began in small churches, then went to larger ones and finally to the largest churches. Although Lowell was giving of himself totally, I could tell something was gnawing on him.

Connie Lundstrom

There was a great concern in my heart that we were missing a tremendous number of people by holding our rallies and crusades in specific churches. We held revivals in many denominational churches, but no matter how I tried I couldn't shake the feeling that we weren't reaching as many as we could. Nine out of 10 people wouldn't attend certain churches because of the label over the door.

My ministry has always been straight salvation. The message over and over has been, "Give your heart to God and make Jesus Christ Lord of your life!" I felt that if we could just get to neutral buildings such as civic auditoriums we could greatly increase the effectiveness of our ministry.

We had a different philosophy of advertising for the meetings than most churches did in those days. We believed we could increase attendance by placing ads in the newspapers and on radio to announce the coming meetings. The Lord enabled us to get into neutral auditoriums. We started out by having Saturday-night music rallies.

Lowell

LITTLE did I know eight years ago that my life would change as a result of going to a Lundstrom meeting. Lowell was holding a rally in Ada, Minnesota, and I went out to hear him. I was a nightclub entertainer and I heard Lowell was pretty good on the guitar. Nobody bothered to tell me he was also a pretty good preacher. My, he was persuasive, and I gave my heart to Christ that very night.

Chet Priewe
Crusade director for the Lundstroms

Soon, pastors from several different denominations began to attend our meetings. They would say, "Lowell, you preach the Gospel right down the middle of the road. If you will come to our city, we will sponsor your meeting."

Lowell

SEVEN years ago, Lowell and the Lundstroms came to Willmar, Minnesota, for a crusade. Our marriage was on the rocks; it was just about gone. My wife and I gave our hearts to Christ that night, and after that we had a special place in our hearts for the Lundstroms.

Whenever they would be within 100 miles we would take everyone we could think of to the meeting. People were saved because they heard the Gospel through the singing and preaching.

Ed Arness
Director of planned giving for the
Lundstrom ministry

I met the Reverend Jack Trosen in a city-wide crusade. He had driven all the way from Williston, North Dakota, to Sidney, Montana, to invite us to his city. He was pastoring the Holiness Methodist Church in Williston and had heard us on KXEL Radio. Jack was our chairman for our Williston crusade. It was a great meeting. Afterward I asked Jack to join our staff as director of crusades.

Lowell

WHEN Lowell asked me to join the team as crusade director, I told him I would pray about it for a year. I wanted to make sure it was the right decision for everyone concerned. Lowell told me that was okay and if I decided to come he would provide me with a car since I would be on the road a lot.

The year passed, and my wife and four children felt as I did that this was God's will for our lives. Lowell had arranged for me to use a 1957 Ford station wagon, but about a month before I arrived it was demolished.

One of my first tasks after arriving was to find a car body at the junkyard and put the motor from the wrecked station wagon into it. I often tell the fellows who come to work with me to count themselves fortunate that they have a newer car and that they didn't have to overhaul it before they could drive it!

> Jack Trosen
> *Crusade director*

LOWELL hired me to serve as photographer for his prison tour two years ago. I thought he was hiring me for the photos I could take, but Lowell had it in mind for me to be exposed to the Gospel for a week.

Well, it worked. While I was photographing the service at Leavenworth Federal Prison, I joined several of the inmates in making a commitment to Christ. When the inmates stood up to accept salvation, I stood up under the pretense of photographing them. Actually I was giving my life to Christ right then.

Reuben Njaa
Photographer

WHEN I started work with the Lundstroms, I thought to myself, "They will never be able to keep up the fast pace they're going now." That was nine years ago and they are still going strong. Lowell is completely sold out to winning people to Christ and doing it in the most effective ways possible.

One of the things that have impressed me most about Lowell in all these years is his determination to never turn down a request for a rally or crusade, no matter how small the town might be. It has always been his policy to go wherever there were Christian people willing to do the necessary groundwork.

Jack Trosen

LOWELL always wants to help people out. We had scheduled one-nighters for an entire year in our effort to get the new bus. We were staying in this home and Lowell received a phone call from a minister who asked what we were doing for spring vacation. We try to schedule a week's vacation for the team in the spring and one week in the fall. Well, Lowell couldn't say "No," and gave away our spring vacation. We decided to retire for the night, and a few minutes later the phone rang again. Within five minutes he had given away our fall vacation as well. Lowell is good that way, giving away vacations, but it's hard to be upset with him. He looks at it this way: If we were off five nights, 80 to 100 people per night could have given their heart to the Lord had we been on a rally tour. That's 500, maybe even as many as 700 people we could have reached in the week's time.

Gloria Lundstrom

LOWELL is an intense individual, and when he's preaching or communicating with the people he doesn't like to be disturbed. One night in Hillsdale, Michigan, Lowell was making the offering appeal and he became increasingly disturbed by the noise generated by the guitar amplifiers. As he was talking, he walked over to the amplifiers and pulled the jacks out. When he had completed his speech, he called the musicians to the stage to play their number while the people gave their offerings.

The musicians hit the first notes and nothing happened. Bill Simmons whispered to Larry, "Plug me in, plug me in," and there was a general state of panic on the stage. Lowell, forgetting he had unplugged several of the guitars, started giving us hand signals and high signs. When that didn't get a response, he cupped his hands and in a loud whisper demanded, "Play, you dogs!" One of the mikes picked it up, and it was clearly heard in the audience. The whole place fell apart with laughter. The "dogs" business was a private joke among us, but that night we had to share it with the entire crowd.

Larry Strom
Former crusade director

8.

Prime-Time Gospel

LOWELL has so much energy. His mind goes 24 hours a day. I used to think I was a fast mover and could think all the time, but I stopped and rested once in a while.

Lowell came through Des Moines one morning about three o'clock. It was a stormy, blizzardy morning. The telephone rang and I groped for the light switch. When I answered, the voice on the other end said cheerfully, "Hi, Don." There was no mistaking who it was. I asked Lowell where he was, and he told me he was at the large truck stop outside of town. He said he had recorded a new song and he wanted me to hear it. I yawned and asked him how long he was going to be there, and he said about an hour. He asked me if I would come on out and hear it and I said, "Lowell, that's a 45-minute drive from here, one way." He said he would wait.

I got out of bed and my wife asked me where I was going. She looked on, unbelieving, as I told her I was going out to a truck stop to hear a record.

I finally arrived and met Lowell. He had a portable tape recorder and said, "Come on in here," motioning toward the restroom. He put the tape on his recorder and turned the volume way up high so some of the truckers could hear it. I asked him to turn it down. He said, "No, no, just listen." Pretty soon some truckers came in and asked us to "Shut that thing off," but Lowell just kept on playing it. Three more guys came in and gave us a similar greeting. Actually they told us if we didn't turn it down they'd throw us out of there, but Lowell let it play until the song was over. Then he asked me if I thought we could use it in the next TV Special. I told him it was a nice song and I thought we might but let's wait to see how the story went. He got into his bus and headed out, and I made the return 45 minute trip back home. I got there about five o'clock.

Lowell's working day starts about midnight. If he has to make a phone call, he does. I don't mind it, and this was one of the funniest, most unforgettable experiences of our friendship.

Don Thompson
Mark IV Pictures

LOWELL has done a good job with his ministry. I've attended some of his reunions and he handles himself well. He is sincere and it shows. I have been

impressed and pleased to see the Lundstroms doing TV Specials. He and his entire ministry team
look good on TV.

Lowell was in my printing plant recently and we
got to talking about TV. He mentioned the possibil-
ity of a weekly telecast and I told him, "Lowell, if
you're going into that medium, do it while you still
have hair on your head and no wrinkles on that
face of yours." He laughed and said, "Jack, I think I
understand what you mean."

Seriously, Lowell has the message and with his
fine team presents it very well. I think they can use
television very effectively to minister the Gospel to
people.

Jack Adams

YOU never have to guess at what Lowell
means—no reading between the lines. He's right
up front with it. He was thinking about producing a
TV Special and he'd seen the Merle Haggard Special out on the West Coast. He liked the approach
and was looking for someone who could incorpo-
rate some of the ideas on that particular show into
his TV Special. Someone in Hollywood mentioned
my name but Lowell had never heard of me. He
said if he had never heard of me I couldn't be too
good.

I'll never forget how I became acquainted with
Lowell the first time. It was about 11:00 p.m. and
the phone rang at my home. Lowell introduced
himself and asked me if I had ever heard of him. I

told him "No," and there was this three-second pause on the other end of the line, so that put us on an even keel immediately.

He wanted me to do a TV Special and I simply refused. He asked me why, and I told him that people call our company frequently with similar requests but they don't realize what is involved. I said that if he was not going first-class I wasn't going to waste my time because I had other projects in which I was involved. I talked to him for 30 minutes telling him why I didn't want to do it, but he asked me to pray about it. What can you say when a guy lays it before you like that?

So I prayed and prayed about it until I felt very strongly that God wanted us to do it. Finally I said, "Yes," and it has been a tremendous association ever since. I try to save money for the ministry in the productions without taking away from the Special in any way. I look to the Lord for direction on Lowell's Specials. I know the kind of man Lowell is and how intent he is on producing something that will project the Gospel most effectively.

He cares so much about winning people to Christ that one evening in a service he turned around to the camera crew and said, "No more cameras." He wanted to forget the TV production and win the lost souls that were present. Fortunately for the crew, they had just finished for the night. I have produced eight TV Specials for Lowell since our initial effort. I have a very high regard for these people.

Don Thompson

One time we were getting ready to film a portion of a TV Special, a Saturday-night rally in Freeport, Illinois. The high school had never been used for public Christian meetings, but because it was a united crusade and so many churches were cooperating, the principal couldn't deny us on the basis of religion; this was a non-sectarian effort. He had to find some other excuse.

We needed to set up chairs on the floor in order to get the right look for the cameras. The TV Special was riding on what we would film at this meeting.

The principal said, "We absolutely cannot let you plug into our electricity." I said, "That's fine, we'll bring in a generator of our own." We found one by contacting the power company. Then he said, "We cannot allow you to put chairs on the gymnasium floor because they would leave marks." I said, "That's okay—we will cover the floor with plastic silo covering." He said, "No, that's not thick enough."

I said, "Do I understand that the reason we can't put chairs on the floor is because we might make marks?" He replied, "Yes, that is the reason."

I could feel that the devil was working in this and trying to disrupt our meeting and TV shooting schedule, so I said, "I'll eliminate all of your problems. I'll call the largest dealer in floor coverings in this city, and we'll carpet the entire floor of the gym." He said, "You wouldn't do that," so I got on his phone and called the carpet company. I wasn't going to give up the TV Special because of the excuses he had been making up.

The carpet man arrived shortly and measured the gymnasium to determine the number of yards we would need. It was going to cost several thousand dollars. The principal, realizing that I had called his hand, turned to me grudgingly and said, "I'll give you 200 chairs, and that's it!" Then he turned and walked away. We praised the Lord for the victory!

Lowell

WE traveled and slept in the same bus with Lowell and Connie for awhile. Joyce and I would be in our bunk on the bus trying to get some sleep. Lowell would get inspired around two or three o'clock in the morning. He'd come to our bunk, pull back the curtain and say, "Sonny, get the guitar and come quickly. I have just written a song." I'd have to fumble around in the dark, find my slacks and get the guitar and go to the front of the bus where we wouldn't disturb the others. We'd sit up there for two or three hours to complete the song arrangement.

When he's working on a song, Lowell isn't aware of anything else around him. He has the ability to zero-in on whatever he is doing.

Bill Simmons

We were preparing for a recent TV Special, but I had been so busy preaching and traveling that I hadn't had time to write songs. One night, a few days prior to the taping, we had to have all the new songs written. That night I didn't have any songs or strength to write them.

I knelt down to pray, and as I was having devotions God gave me a song for Lisa to sing. I jumped up and completed the song in just a few minutes. Then I prepared to go to bed. As I knelt in prayer, I thanked the Lord for the song. While I was thanking Him, He gave me another song. I reached for a tape recorder and completed that one. I knelt by my bedside and thanked the Lord once again. Yet another song came into my heart and mind. I arose and completed that song too. This happened four more times before the night was over. The next morning I had six songs ready for recording the TV Special. For a boy from Peever, South Dakota (a small town south of Sisseton where the Lundstroms grew up), six songs in one night was unquestionably a miracle.

Lowell

9.

Sisseton, U.S.A.

I remember when the Lundstroms' Message for America ministry started in Madge's living room. She would work day and night to take care of the work that needed to be done.

Carl Johnson

WHEN Madge prayed that prayer about helping Lowell in his ministry, she meant it. Pretty soon she had quite a bit of work to do and there would be papers spread out all over our living room. She added a girl and then another, and Jack Trosen joined the team as crusade director. Soon there wasn't even enough room for us to live in our kitchen. They would answer letters, send out thank-you letters and print that little newsletter on the old mimeograph machine. It was a growing ministry.

Lawrence Lundstrom

TWO of the people who have contributed much to the success of the ministry have been Madge and Lawrence Lundstrom. They actually met with a great deal of hardship in their life to handle their farming operation, let alone the headquarters for a growing ministry. I have never known two people who have dedicated themselves more sincerely to the efforts of the present generation. Most parents their age would want to sit back and enjoy a little bit of time to themselves. Madge and Lawrence are in their 60s and they work harder every year.

Harold Torness

LOWELL'S mom is kind of the Golda Meir around here, a legend in her own time. I deeply appreciate her strength and tenacity of spirit and character. It's an experience in learning, just listening to her share of the life she and Lawrence had starting out on the farm and in the early days of the ministry.

Bruce Schoeman
Projects director

AT one time the site of the Lundstrom Message for America headquarters was planned as an industrial park. Our dream was to encourage a large manufacturing firm to come to Sisseton and employ local citizens. We had a group develop the concept and look for new businesses. This was more of a challenge than we had anticipated. We found ourselves settling for smaller businesses including an auto dealership, a car wash and a farm implement company.

Lowell's ministry had just about taken over Madge and Lawrence's entire house; so when one of the businesses in the industrial park area dissolved, Message for America bought the building and converted it into outstanding, functional headquarters.

Somehow the committee trying to attract industry thought it had failed until they realized that the ministry now employs 60 to 65 full-time people. The Lundstrom ministry is one of the major employers of the community.

Harold Torness

I'VE been involved with this thing right from the very beginning. I can remember our first board meeting. We figured out our budget and determined we needed to raise $50,000 to meet the expenses of the coming year. It looked like an impossible task.

Carl Johnson

LOWELL claims Sisseton as his home, which is fine for us. Both Lowell and Connie refer to that freely on radio and television. A lot of people wouldn't want to be associated with such a small town.

Lowell is the finest Chamber of Commerce material we've got. He's kind of like Joe Robbie, owner of the Miami Dolphins, who is from around here.

Between the two of them they draw the attention to Sisseton and we're indebted to them for that.
Jack Adams

IT'S quite something when you can produce people like the Lundstroms out of your own community and have them stay right there. It's unusual that people of humble backgrounds have come to this station in life. They are heard and seen by millions of people and have a great following of Christian folks who love them and support their ministry.

Several years ago Lowell, seeing the revenue increasing each year, grew concerned that some people might question the use of the money and how it was handled. He took all of the property that had been in his name and turned it over to the ministry—the buses, instruments, everything. He also insisted on a regular annual audit by an outside firm. He didn't want anyone to say that donations were going directly to him.

As secretary-treasurer of Message for America and a longtime volunteer, I can attest that this is the most conscientious organization I have ever had the privilege of serving. A seven-man board of directors provides guidance for the entire operation.

Lowell receives a nominal salary which is about $6000 a year lower than that received by the street sweepers of San Francisco. He's happy with it, knowing that more money can go directly into the outreach for those in need of salvation.
Carl Johnson

AS a banker, I can say the ministry has fulfilled every responsibility it has been asked to do, and the association has been good business for the bank. Oftentimes people are suspicious of religious organizations that are doing a lot and searching for financial support with which to spread the Gospel. From my perspective as president of this bank, I am aware of the tremendous costs and the pressure of the communications industry and how much money it takes to put TV Specials and radio programs on the air.

One assurance folks who support the Lundstroms should have is that I have never been able to recognize even one extravagance. Lowell, Larry and Leon have modest tastes, live in modest homes and drive lower-priced cars. None of them has personally profited to a degree that would be comparable to what most of us would expect for working as hard as they do.

I think the entire state of South Dakota owes the Lundstroms a debt of gratitude. In 1976, as a member of the Glacial Lakes Association, I was confronted with the question of what significant contribution South Dakota could make to our country's bicentennial celebration. While in the meeting, I suddenly remembered I had seen two or three TV Specials produced by the Lundstroms and it occurred to me that they could do a fine job of representing our state. The Glacial Lakes Association discussed it with the governor. He had also seen one of Lowell's Specials and he endorsed the idea.

The Lundstroms produced the TV Special, "Movin' thru Dakota Country," which became the one outstanding promotion of 1976.

Harold Torness

10.

Fishers of Men—
The Lundstrom Team

I made a comment to Lowell which bears repeating. The type of people he has attracted to work with him has been most unusual. He has surrounded the Lundstrom headquarters with very superior personnel.

Couples who come here to work with Lowell and his group make outstanding contributions to the community. Their families are active in their various churches and a real asset to the community.

Harold Torness

I have had the privilege of knowing many of the people who work at the Lundstrom headquarters and those who travel with the ministry team. To

keep people of that caliber contented to be in a town this size is quite something!
Jack Adams

In a year's time, the Lundstroms minister to approximately 250,000 persons in public rallies, prison appearances and Family-Life seminars. This figure doesn't include the uncounted numbers touched through radio, church family camps, schools and nursing homes.

More than thirty million people have seen the Lundstrom TV Specials across America. Our tremendous support team in Sisseton and the dedicated ministry team, along with literally thousands of our friends who contribute, continue to make this outreach possible.

The ministry team travels more than sixty-five thousand miles by bus each year. Our crusade directors and personnel travel nearly two hundred thousand miles by plane and car to arrange for our crusades, rallies and other outreach ministries. Our MESSAGE Magazine goes to nearly one hundred thousand homes, and our sermons on cassette tapes and records and other outreach materials reach hundreds of thousands each year throughout this country. Around twelve thousand men, women and young people receive Christ as their Savior in our services each year. We thank God for His rich blessing on our efforts.

Lowell

AS pilot for the Lundstroms and their crusade staff, I have to fly in some pretty rough weather from time to time in order to get Lowell and the team to the crusades. One night Lowell, Connie and I were flying out of Duluth, Minnesota, in a single-engine plane. We were flying into some icing conditions.

I was trying to get above the altitude causing the icing. I had asked Lowell to hold a flashlight out the window at the wing to check on the ice condition. When I asked him to do that it didn't go over very well. He just told me to keep an eye on it and tell him how it turned out. We could hear ice sputtering off the propeller and when he finally got on the ground and saw all the ice melting and falling off the wings he said, "It doesn't make any difference what it costs, we are getting a twin-engine aircraft with wing de-icers."

Joe Gruber
Pilot

WHEN I was a little girl, 8 years old, I remember praying that God would help me go to Bible school and be in a Gospel singing group. I wanted to serve the Lord and be in a ministry of music. Well, the Lord heard that earnest child's prayer, and I feel blessed to be part of this outreach effort.

My own children are having a part in our ministry now. Both of our daughters, LaDawn and LaShawn, regularly sing in the rallies, meetings and TV Specials. We have a little son now, Lee Donavan, and I know it won't be long before he will find a place in the ministry. Isn't God good to give you the desires of your heart?

Gloria Lundstrom

DAD was in a bind. He had looked everywhere for a pianist to replace Steve Booher, who had decided to go home for a while. One day we had a program for a group at the Crippled Children's Home in Jamestown, North Dakota. After Steve left the stage, I went up on stage and started playing "How Great Thou Art" on the piano. Dad knew Steve had left the stage area and looked around to see who was playing. He was so startled to see me playing that he yelled, "Play it again, play it again!" I played it again and he said, "Do it again, do it again!"

That was how I began my career as the Lundstroms' pianist. There was never the question, "Londa, do you think you can handle it?" Dad just knew I would be the pianist. I was 10 years old then and I have been the pianist for five years now.

I never had any formal training. Steve Booher showed me a few chords and Dad taught me some basic chord patterns from what he knew on the guitar. I used to watch Steve closely as he played, where he put his fingers on the keys of the piano— that was it. I don't take any credit for my playing because the Lord gave me the talent. I thank Him for it all the time.

Londa Lundstrom
Pianist

I'VE been with the Lundstroms as sound technician since 1974. I became involved with the local arrangements committee in Billings, Montana, when the Lundstroms came to our city to conduct a meeting. During the crusade I noticed their sound equipment was in very poor repair, so I brought my tool box and began to mend it. They had a sound board to mix instruments and voices, but no one knew how to run it. I operated it for them during the crusade. Near the end of the crusade, Lowell asked me to join the team.

I have many duties on the road, but my main function is to run the sound board, keep all the equipment in good repair and replace worn-out components before they become a problem during a concert or rally.

John Poore
Sound technician

IT'S great to have children involved in the ministry, especially the singing. They add such a tremendous dimension of sincerity and pure enthusiasm. Lisa has been doing solos for several years now, and Lowell Jr. enjoys the opportunity to sing out every chance he gets. With our little boy, Lance, and Gloria and Ronda's little ones, we have a new generation of Lundstrom singers on the way. We praise God for the children and the lessons we learn from them.

Connie Lundstrom

Traveling and living with 17 full-time people in two buses is not the easiest thing in the world, but they are all dedicated to the Lord. Everyone does his share and that's what makes this thing work smoothly 300 days out of the year that we are on the road.

Lowell

11.

You Guys Really Are for Real

WHEN you've been out on the road for a month or two, ministering night after night, it is hard to keep giving your best. This is especially true if the crowd is small or doesn't react to our ministry.

Lowell is the leader, and he encourages us to read our Bibles and pray every day. He stays close to the Lord, and it is a joy to see how he inspires not only the crowds who come but the entire ministry team. He is a hard man to keep up with because of his energy and he pushes us to the limit, but we love him with all our hearts and know what motivates him. He is totally dedicated to winning people to Christ.   Bill Simmons

LOWELL definitely knows what he's doing and what he wants to do. He works exceptionally hard at it. Lowell is very diligent and always has been.

He never slacks off. When he was a kid working for me, he never dragged his shirt any time I know of. He's still putting in those long hours every day. I don't know of anybody else who would work so hard for as little money as he makes. I am confident that he is one of God's servants.

Les Stillson

BECAUSE of Lowell's straightforward blood-and-guts drive on any project, one of his former musicians told him, "Lowell, you would make a tremendous Communist." Praise God, Lowell's commitment and energy are dedicated to Christ.

Seeing him operate in so many different situations where things happen fast with little time to get the job done, I wonder how he can do it.

I think he would have made a great commander for one of David's special task forces we read about in the Old Testament. I'm sure Lowell would not come back without a successful accomplishment in the duty he was assigned.

Bruce Schoeman

BEING a member of a traditional denomination, I have not seen our church use radio and television. Through my friendship with Lowell, I have come to realize that it is an important part of any earnest ministry today.

Lowell uses radio and television effectively, speaking in down-to-earth terms and using contemporary music to reach people the staid churches would miss.

What amazes me is the fact that his ministry has attracted so many people from all age groups. In his meetings I see teen-agers and many young married couples with families. Lowell has always been attentive to older persons and had good audience reception for a wide range of ages.

Harold Torness

NOWADAYS you hear about ministries going off the road or quitting. Lowell has always had his goal set. He knows what he has been called to do. He never gets discouraged. He always seems to know where he is supposed to be. What a fantastic encouragement he is to the people who travel with him!

Joyce Simmons
Wife of Bill Simmons

THE secret to my brother's success is this: as a preacher and as an individual, Lowell follows the Spirit of God like a hound on the trail of a rabbit. He senses the need and follows the Holy Spirit, and he'll never go far off the trail. He'll just keep on sniffing at it and come right back until he'll have a person treed, you might say, and lead him to a face-to-face confrontation with Jesus Christ. He'll give him all the information and an opportunity to make a commitment to Jesus Christ.

Larry Lundstrom

WHEN Bill and I first joined the ministry team, our son was just 8 or 9 days old. During the night I would have to get up on the bus and feed him.

Many nights I got up I would find Lowell down on his knees reading his Bible and praying. It was an inspiration to all of us to know he would be praying in the midnight hours.

Joyce Simmons

WHAT impressed me about Lowell is that his goal is not to win 10,000 souls. Lowell's goal is not to win a million. His goal is to win everyone that God brings to him.

Larry Strom

THE beautiful thing about Lowell's presentation of the Gospel is his masterful use of truth and humor. I would liken it to a nurseryman planting a tree. He'll step on that spade and press it as far into the ground as it will go. Then he'll kind of lean back on that spade until the soil airs out a little bit. Then he'll take another stomp on it.

Well, Lowell takes a stomp down on that spade, trying to win a person for the Lord. He'll stomp down with some Biblical truth, then lean back just a little with some well-timed humor so he can take another stab down. He uses truth and humor to win people to the Lord. I consider Lowell a genius of persuasion not only on the platform but in individual counseling siuations. He will help a person establish a relationship with Christ through observations, references to his personal experience and through logical persuasion. Lowell devours newspapers and periodicals every day and has knowledge of life-situations to draw on. That is a tremendous asset to his logical, persuasive approach to helping people who need answers to life's problems.

Bruce Schoeman

If anything has been able to help me advance in the ministry, it is the overwhelming determination to move ahead and do God's will. Although I am very plain and common, I try to learn from each incident that comes into my life. I try to see how I can be more effective.

Some people have great charisma all by themselves. I don't have that. The only charisma I have is when the Lord anoints me by His Spirit to do a particular task. Then I don't feel inferior to any situation or problem. I just know that I am totally equipped through His anointing and His Spirit.

We travel 300 nights a year and unload, set up, tear down and load back onto the buses about three tons of equipment every day. Then we travel half the night to get to our next destination and do it all over again. To keep up this pace is a spiritual, physical and logistical miracle.

This ministry is really just a band of ordinary people doing what has become their specialty. There are greater singers than the Lundstroms and there are greater musicians. There are many with a lot more natural talent than we have, but I don't think there is anyone with any greater determination and dedication to do the

Lord's work. Each one does his particular work as unto the Lord. This makes for a smoothrunning organization. The Lord is in the middle of this ministry. When He blesses the plain, it becomes supernatural!

When our first pianist, Steve Booher, came with us we were on the road doing rallies every night. After about six weeks of watching and careful examination, Steve turned to me one day and said, "Lowell, you guys really are for real." I told him I was glad he finally realized that.

First Corinthians 1:26-28 reads, "For you see your calling, brethren, how that not many wise men after the flesh, not many mighty, not many noble, are called; but God hath chosen the foolish things of the world to confound the wise; and God hath chosen the weak things of the world to confound the things which are mighty; and base things of the world, and things which are despised, hath God chosen, yea, and things which are of naught to bring to naught things that are."

As I look at our ministry, we have all the Biblical qualifications. We are foolish, we are weak and we are "of naught," so God has chosen to take and use us. Someone who is nothing but completely committed to God is greater than someone who is everything without His blessing. The strongest point of our ministry is the fact that we are very plain yet committed to Jesus Christ, our Lord and Savior.

Lowell

12.

"My Dad's the Greatest:" Lowell the Family-Man

I'VE always been so proud of Lowell because he takes time with the children, even as busy as he is. The time he spends with the kids is really quality time. There may not be as much as some fathers spend with their kids, but Lowell makes every minute count. Every day when we're on the road, he's always picking up the baby, hugging the daughters, encouraging them.

Connie Lundstrom

DAD and I have a good relationship, all right. It's hard sometimes because his work is so heavy, but we have a great relationship for a father and daughter. Every week or so, we just lie around and talk for a long time about different things—anything and everything. We talk about what's going on, what I'm progressing in. He's always so busy but he likes to know what's going on in my world.

Lisa Lundstrom

WELL, I think my dad is the greatest dad on earth, like any kid would say. Some special things we do when he has time are hunting, fishing, skiing—a whole bunch of things.

Lowell (Tiny) Lundstrom, Jr.

WE'RE not a normal family, living on a bus and keeping late hours, but this rather unregimented lifestyle is normal to us. During one-night rallies, we're cooped up on the bus day and night, but we have a real good time. We're all very close. We've all got a candid, open relationship. We talk about things and we don't have to worry about what Mom or Dad are going to think. We just say what we feel and Mom and Dad say what they feel. We really communicate.

Londa Lundstrom

EVERY one of our children respects and loves Lowell deeply. Traveling as we do on the bus, they are a part of everything we experience. They are with us when we go through trials, when the bus breaks down, they've been with us through it all. When we needed a new bus, God provided it. It's just tremendous for the children to see this firsthand, how God provides for us on a daily basis. Every morning when the children wake up, they see Lowell praying and reading the Bible. They see

him in the early hours on his knees praying. They see him as he leads daily devotions. I know without a doubt that he's sensitive to the Lord in every area.
Connie Lundstrom

MY dad holds devotions on the bus every day. We read the Bible and pray, and we have a special book that he reads to us out of.
Lowell Lundstrom, Jr.

WE try to have devotions every day. Dad has a real special way. When I read the Bible, as much as I love to read it, a lot of things in the Old Testament are just dry and without too much meaning because I don't know the proper context. Dad has a special way of putting things to make them fun and interesting. Recently, on our way home, Dad read the story of Jezebel and Elijah from 2 Kings. I've heard it many times before, but he told it in such a way that it made me feel like I was actually right there in the middle of it all happening. And that's why people really enjoy him.
Londa Lundstrom

LOWELL isn't one to spare the rod. He believes in firm discipline. We've never had to use it much, once the children have had a dose of his old-fashioned spankings. We have a policy where if they don't mind, they get five swats with a belt. If they misbehave a second time in a given area, they get 10 swats, the third time, 15, the fourth time, 20, etc. Generally, they don't go beyond the first five.
Connie Lundstrom

LIKE my mom says, the swats go up by five every time we do something we shouldn't all over again.
Lowell Lundstrom, Jr.

(Ed. note: Lowell Jr. says it sometimes takes him two times to learn.)

FROM the very beginning, all of us kids have been real independent. We can do basically what we want, but we all know where our limitations are. Just don't cross over that line. When you cross over that line, you're gonna be hung.
Londa Lundstrom

AT my age, Dad mostly just talks to me. He'll show me where I'm wrong, and then he'll back it up with scripture and show me why I shouldn't do it. I think that's better than anything else.
Lisa Lundstrom

SOMETIMES we have a difference of opinion. If, for instance, I'm right and Dad's wrong but he goes ahead and does things his way, he always comes back and says, "I was wrong—you were right." No matter how much he'd like to say he's right, he admits it when he's wrong. He's not perfect and doesn't claim to be, but he always tries to look at things from your point of view, not just his. He makes you feel valuable as a person.
Londa Lundstrom

DAD spends time helping Tiny learn the bass, helping us all with simple things, no matter how boring. He has concern for me as the middle child, not being in the shadow of my sister or brother. National statistics show the first child is more aggressive and the second is not. I'm kind of mellow like my mom. Dad helps me out where it counts.

Lisa Lundstrom

SOMETIMES I feel like having a pity-party. It's normal for a wife to have her husband's attention all the time; but with the ministry, it just can't be. There are many women whose husbands are around them all the time because their jobs don't take them away from home. I read something in a book that has helped me tremendously. It said, "Would you rather be married to 10 percent of a 100-percent man or have 100 percent of a 10-percent man?" Lowell is truly a 100-percent man.

Connie Lundstrom

ONE time my dad took me hunting for geese with my Grampa Lundstrom. It was cold and we were out in a blind. There were about one hundred geese flying in, and I wanted to shoot at the same time Dad and Grampa did. I saw Grampa shoulder his gun. The geese were coming in but they weren't close enough. I was so excited, I started shooting and blew the whole thing. They all flew off. But Dad took me hunting again. I guess he wasn't too upset about it.

Lowell Lundstrom, Jr.

DAD and I have the same kind of quirks. But I got over chewing my finger nails. Dad bribed me with a horse. He said if I'd stop chewing them he'd get me a horse. I stopped and he gave me the horse like he said. Dad still chews his. Once he quit for four months because of a contest with Larry Strohm and Bruce Schoeman. He came in second, but then he started chewing them again. I'd like to help him, but I'm not sure bribing would make it with him.

Lisa Lundstrom

YEH, my dad has a habit of chewing his fingernails. I guess he's under so much pressure that's the only way he gets any relief.

Lowell Lundstrom, Jr.

IF Lowell has a hobby, I'd say it's collecting books. He's a voracious reader. I mean, he has a large library. After every tour we unload books he's bought all over the country. If we're eating in a cafe, Lowell's reading newspapers, books and magazines, keeping up-to-date with what's happening.

Connie Lundstrom

IN the bus all the time, I see Dad reading books on how to help people. He's always reading and praying, trying to find out things about the Lord. It's a constant thing 24 hours a day.

Londa Lundstrom

LOWELL reads every which way. He reads three or four books at a time. He skips through some and reads straight through others. He'll walk through the bus getting everyone's attention. "Hey, listen to this," or, "You've gotta read this book." As a family, we're always swapping books. We all love to read, so we do a lot of sharing.

Connie Lundstrom

I really admire Dad's ability to keep his sanity in this kind of life, to be able to run each and every area. He's trying to put people under him in charge of certain loads, but mostly he has it all on his own. To be able to run a family, to be a boss, a producer, a father and a husband and all these things combined is a hard job.

Lisa Lundstrom

WE seldom can unwind and relax. Dad, I don't think he ever does. If we're home for a day or two, I can always tell he's antsy and know what he's thinking. On a few of those rare days off, I've heard him say, "Man, there could be 150 souls won to Christ tonight." It seems a little ridiculous to me, but that has got him where he is today as a person.

Believe me, he's gotta have the Lord in the center of his life to live like he does. Who ever heard of running this type of organization with 75 people working for you—directing them from 1,000 miles away, calling them from a telephone in a greasy-spoon truckstop where we have stopped to fuel the bus and eat? He's always getting pressure from different people, but he handles it real good.

Londa Lundstrom

WHEN the pressures become so great, humor is Dad's pop-off valve. He and Larry and Leon are absolute comedians when they get together under these circumstances. Dad has a dry sense of humor, and sometimes he keeps us all laughing with an unending stream of funny stories or comments. The humor seems to be a real pressure reliever for him—and us all for that matter.

Londa Lundstrom

PEOPLE seem to have a lot of fun when they hear him speak. He gets his point across, and by the end of the rally they know they've got to give their heart to Christ. God has given him a different approach to the same message of salvation.

Lisa Lundstrom

SOMETIMES I sit behind the organ on stage and say, "Is this really my father that's having a part of winning these thousands of people to Christ?" Sometimes I'm awestruck. It doesn't really feel like he's my dad at the moment because I know it's the Lord working.

Londa Lundstrom

I'VE lived with him and observed him all throughout our ministry, and what amazes me is that day in, day out, Lowell never ceases to minister. After he's preached in the evening, he's back in the counseling area working with individuals. He's genuinely concerned about people. It just seems to be a God-given compassion.

Connie Lundstrom